AMERICAN GOVERNMENT

CLEP* Study Guide

ACE THE CLEP

971121715143

Published by Breely Crush Publishing, LLC
10808 River Front Parkway
South Jordan, UT 84095
www.breelycrushpublishing.com

ISBN-10: 1-61433-285-1
ISBN-13: 978-1-61433-285-5

Printed and bound in the United States of America.

Table of Contents

Introduction

To understand how American government works, one must first understand the history of and reasons for its creation. While the structure of the government may seem unnecessarily complex at first, it was designed that way for a purpose.

After the American Revolution, the Founding Fathers of the government faced the task of putting together a new form of government that would protect the rights of all its citizens and would give a previously unheard of level of freedom to most of them (not all groups of citizens were initially given these freedoms). In order to accomplish this goal, the Founding Fathers developed the idea of a Democratic Republic.

In a Democratic Republic, the ruler of the people and all other political leaders are selected by the people by majority vote. The uniqueness of the American system was the combination of these two ideas.

Democracies were not new. The term democracy comes from the joining of two Greek words: demos (people) and kratos (strength). Ancient Greece was the world's first democracy because all-important issues were voted on directly by its citizens. Even though the United States consisted of only 13 states at the time, the Founding Fathers realized that the same type of direct voting by the people would not be possible because of the country's large size and growing population. Instead, they developed the concept of a representative democracy.

A representative democracy allows the citizens to vote for individuals who will work on their behalf to make the laws and decisions that influence their lives. While they don't vote on specific issues, the idea is that those representatives will be influenced in their voting by the desires and wishes of the people who elected them.

History of the Constitution

When the thirteen states decided to break free of the rule of Great Britain in 1776, their representatives in the Second Continental Congress (the First Continental Congress had lasted from September 5, 1774 to May 10, 1775 but did not include representatives from all thirteen colonies) decided to express their desire in writing.

The Second Continental Congress selected five men to prepare what would be known as the Declaration of Independence. Thomas Jefferson composed the document, and his approach was heavily influenced by John Locke. Locke (1632 – 1704) was a British philosopher and the author of Two Treatises on Government. While his philosophies about politics would have a tremendous impact on the Constitution and the American government, it was three of his ideas that are most prominent in the Declaration of Independence.

One of those ideas is that there is no "divine right" of kings. Locke believed that God did not choose individuals to be rulers, which was what most monarchs of the time believed. Another of those ideas was that all people are born with the right to "life, liberty, and property." This second idea appeared in the Declaration of Independence as "life, liberty, and the pursuit of happiness."

The third of Locke's influential ideas was that effective governments only exist because of the will of the people who are governed. That meant when the governed were unhappy with the government, they had the right to insist on demolishing the old government in order to replace it with something different. This idea eventually lead to the American Revolution.

At the same time that the Declaration of Independence was being written, the Second Continental Congress was also working on the Articles of Confederation which would be the basis for the country's new government. The Congress debated over the document for 16 months before approving its final form on November 15, 1777. Three years later, the states ratified the Articles of Confederation.

While the Articles of Confederation held the union together during the American Revolution, after the war ended in 1783, their weaknesses became clear. For example, the Articles of Confederation did not include any way of enforcing the collection of taxes and did not address commerce issues between states. Also, changes to the Articles required unanimous consent from all of the states, but many states would not send their representatives to the meetings, which meant the government could not accomplish anything.

The problems with the Articles and the current method of government were clear, so in 1787 a committee of 55 delegates met for five months with the intention of putting together a new set of guidelines for the government. They began working on what became the United States Constitution.

Original Contents of the Constitution

The contents of the Constitution were impacted by the need for a compromise between the states. Two plans for the structure of the government were developed during the Constitutional Conventional and both had support from the some of the states.

One of those plans was called the Virginia Plan. In the plan, the Congress would be bicameral. The number of representatives in both houses would be based on a state's population, but only the Lower House would be elected by the people. The other House would be selected by members of the Lower House.

The second plan was known as the New Jersey Plan. It called for a unicameral Congress made up of an equal number of representatives from each state. These delegates would be elected by the people in those states.

Neither plan was used. Instead, the Connecticut Compromise was reached. The Compromise allowed for the creation of a bicameral Congress. The number of representatives for one House would be based on the population of each state (House of Representatives) while each state would send two representatives to the other House (Senate). Another part of the compromise was that the Representatives would be elected through direct elections while the Senators would be appointed by the legislative bodies of each state.

This compromise illustrated one of the important principles outlined in the Constitution: the equality of every state. However, that was only one principle. There were a number of others as well:

- All people are equal under the law
- The government can be changed by changing the Constitution
- No person is above the law
- The Constitution is the supreme law of the land
- There must be a separation of power

This final principle was considered critical to the success of the Constitution because it would prohibit any one branch of government from becoming more powerful.

According to the Constitution, there were to be three branches of government: the executive (the president), the legislative (the Congress), and the judicial (the Supreme Court). Each branch would have different powers and would watch over the other two branches through a system of checks and balances.

When the original draft of the Constitution was completed, it contained only the preamble and seven articles which outlined the principles discussed above. The entire document was only about 4000 words in length when it was submitted to the states for ratification in September 1787.

Constitutional Additions

When the Constitution went before the states for approval, it found both praise and criticism. The Federalists, including Alexander Hamilton and James Madison, believed it should be ratified and wrote a series of 85 letters explaining the benefits and advantages of the government it proposed.

The Anti-Federalists, such as Patrick Henry and James Monroe, did not agree. They believed the Constitution gave too much power to the central government while weakening the power of the states. They were also concerned that such a strong central government may erode the basic rights to freedom which had been promised to citizens in the Declaration of Independence.

In order to gain the support of Anti-Federalists, it was agreed that a Bill of Rights would be added to the Constitution in order to ensure that did not happen.

The Bill of Rights was officially added to the Constitution in 1791, which was two years after the document was ratified and put into effect in 1789. The new section contained ten amendments and those were soon followed by a number of additional amendments.

The idea of allowing changes and additions to the Constitution in the form of amendments was a challenging one. Its authors recognized that if it was to last, it would need to be adaptable to changes in society, especially as the population of the United States continued to grow. However, they did not want to make the amendment process so simple that changes would be made without careful consideration. They also wanted to be sure that the process of change was not so rigid that it would prohibit necessary amendments from being made simply because a unanimous decision could not be reached.

Taking all of that into consideration, the authors decided on an amendment process which allows for modifications in two ways. The most common way is through the Supreme Court. The job of the Supreme Court is to interpret the meaning of the Constitution and to apply it to actual situations. Through their interpretations, the meaning of the different passages within the Constitution has changed over the years.

The second method of change is by formally introducing a new amendment to the Constitution. To start the process, two-thirds of the Senate and the House of Representatives must vote to approve the amendment. For the amendment to be added to the Constitution, three-fourths of the states must vote to approve it as well. As a result, only 17 amendments have been added to the Constitution since the Bill of Rights was introduced.

Below is a list of the amendments, the date they were added, and a brief description of what each contains. The first ten made up the Bill of Rights.

Amendment I (1791) – Guarantees freedom of speech, of the press, and of religion. It also guarantees the rights of citizens to assemble and to petition the government for change.

Amendment II (1791) – Guarantees the right of citizens to bear arms.

Amendment III (1791) – Guarantees that no one will be forced to house soldiers during peacetime.

Amendment IV (1791) – Protects citizens against "unreasonable searches and seizures."

Amendment V (1791) – Protects citizens from being held without criminal charges, from having to testify against themselves, from being tried for the same crime twice (double jeopardy), and from being deprived of their rights without due process.

Amendment VI (1791) – Ensures the rights of each citizen to a public trial and the right to an attorney. It also guarantees the individual the right to know the charges against them.

Amendment VII (1791) – Guarantees the right to a jury trial in all cases involving more than $20.

Amendment VIII (1791) – Protects individuals from "cruel or unusual punishment" and from excessive bail.

Amendment IX (1791) – Explains that even though some rights are not listed in the Constitution that does not mean individuals do not have those rights.

Amendment X (1791) – Gives power to the states to deal with anything that is not covered in the Constitution.

Amendment XI (1795) – Prohibits a citizen of one state from suing another state and prevents foreign individuals from suing states.

Amendment XII (1804) – Discusses the election process for President and Vice-president.

Amendment XIII (1865) – Abolishes slavery.

Amendment XIV (1868) – Guarantees citizenship for people born in the United States or for people who go through the naturalization process, provides equal protection for all people under the law, and prevents states from denying a citizen their rights without due process.

Amendment XV (1870) – Guarantees the rights of all men, regardless of color, to vote.

Amendment XVI (1913) – Gives the government the right to collect income tax.

Amendment XVII (1913) – Allows for the direct election of Senators.

Amendment XVIII (1919) – Prohibits the making, selling, and transporting of alcohol.

Amendment XIX (1920) – Gives women the right to vote.

Amendment XX (1933) – Deals with specifics of when presidential and congressional terms begin.

Amendment XXI (1933) – Repeals Amendment XVIII.

Amendment XXII (1951) – Prevents a president from serving more than two terms.

Amendment XXIII (1961) – Allows the District of Columbia the right to vote for president.

Amendment XXIV (1964) – Prohibits the charging of a poll tax.

Amendment XXV (1967) – Discusses the succession of the president and vice-president.

Amendment XXVI (1971) – Allows people to vote at 18, instead of at 21.

Amendment XXVII (1992) – Places a limit on how often Congress can vote to raise their pay.

One constitutional clause that has played a significant role in the development of the United States political structure is the Supremacy Clause. This clause states that the Constitution is the "supreme law of the land." In practice, the Supremacy Clause has been interpreted to mean that the powers of the federal government are higher than the powers of state governments. When the laws or actions of the two come into conflict then the legal right of the federal government will overcome that of the state. As a result, any laws passed by local governments must be in harmony with federal regulations.

The Declaration of Independence

No document in American history can compare with the Declaration of Independence in the place that it holds in the minds and hearts of American citizens. It is not only critical to any exploration of the growth of democracy in the United States, it is in many ways the root document of that democracy. We begin here, for the Declaration sheds its light both backward, to illuminate the development of democratic ideas and institutions in the New World, and forward, to indicate the ways in which the United States has lived up to the promise of the Declaration as well as those areas in which the ideas have taken longer to mature.

It is important to understand that the Declaration of Independence is far more than an announcement that thirteen English colonies perched on the eastern seaboard of North America considered themselves freed of allegiance to Great Britain and to its King, George III. In it we can find the key ideas about how the Americans of that generation thought a free people should live, what form their government should take, and what the mutual responsibilities were between a government and its citizens in order that both order and liberty could be sustained.

In 1763, when the great war between France and Great Britain for the control of the North American empire ended, if one walked down the street of any colonial town or village, or stopped along a rural road at a farm, and asked the residents what they considered themselves to be, they would not have answered, "We are Americans." Instead, they would have proudly declared themselves His Majesty's loyal subjects living in the colonies. They saw themselves as sharing with their cousins in the Mother Country a common language, common culture and traditions and, above all, a common body of legal rights and privileges.

The French and Indian Wars, which eliminated France as a power in the New World and greatly increased the security of the British colonies, also left His Majesty's Government with an enormous debt. In looking at their prosperous colonies across the ocean, English officials decided that, at the least, the colonists ought to pay the cost of their own government and security. As Great Britain attempted to strengthen its control over the commerce and government of the colonies in the 1760s in order to raise revenue, one writer after another protested that such measures violated the colonists' rights as Englishmen.

In fact, the very distance of the colonies had already altered those rights, as well as the perceptions of the colonists regarding rights of the individual in general. The frontier society of the American colonies had fostered a greater sense of individual autonomy, a sense that government should not interfere in the daily lives of its citizens, and that the purpose of government is to secure and protect the liberty and property of its citizens. The seeds of these ideas clearly could be found in English thought, but British government and law in the eighteenth century were slowly changing to give the King, and especially Parliament, greater authority. Law, according to Sir William Blackstone, was the command of the sovereign.

Americans, however, rejected the ideas of strong governments and authoritarian sovereigns, claiming that they went against British traditions of rights. The pamphlets that began to appear in the colonies in the early 1760s attacked the growing power of Parliament and warned that such increased authority would undermine their individual liberties. As England tried to tighten its imperial controls, it found a strong vein of resistance in the colonies. Efforts to impose taxes were met by protests, boycotts and petitions, and for the most part the Crown's efforts proved futile. In the early 1770s royal government in the colonies disintegrated, so that by 1775 the real ruling powers in the colonies were the locally elected legislatures. These assemblies had relatively clear notions about what government ought and ought not to do, and to a large extent Americans in all the colonies shared these views. The enduring importance of the Declaration of Independence derives in part from its authors' ability to capture and articulate those sentiments.

After its petitions failed to secure redress, the Second Continental Congress voted to declare independence from England, and named John Adams, Benjamin Franklin and Thomas Jefferson to draft a declaration. All three men were familiar with English tradition, and each had thought at length about the problems of government. But of the three, Jefferson was acknowledged to possess the most facile pen, and his words caught the hopes and ideals of the American experiment.

The Declaration of Independence, John Adams later said, had not a single new idea in it. Certainly one can see the influence of John Locke and other English writers in it. But one can also see the notions of government that had been intensely discussed in the colonies in hundreds of pamphlets in the previous fifteen years. The Declaration is clearly part of this pamphlet tradition. It is in fact a pamphlet, a propaganda document designed to justify a radical, unprecedented and unlawful action by placing the blame on a wicked king and Parliament. The colonists, the authors claimed, had done no more than protect their God-given rights.

It would be a mistake, however, to dismiss the Declaration as just a propaganda document, for it is far more than that. It is the culmination of more than a century and a half of colonial life, during which the settlers in North America developed their unique notions of government, a process in which they gradually stopped being Englishmen and became Americans.

The long list of grievances Jefferson marshalled to support his charge that the king had violated his obligations to the people is hardly convincing to a modern reader, and like all good propagandists, Jefferson distorted history to serve his purposes. But if one reads the grievances carefully, they contain notions that are basic to American democracy: government is a compact among the people, and can be overthrown when it fails to fulfill its obligations; government exists to protect the rights and property of its citizens; every person accused of a crime is entitled to trial by a jury of peers; the state cannot search the homes of its citizens without a warrant; and taxes cannot be levied without the consent of the people.

From a constitutional point of view, the Declaration served several purposes. It enshrined the compact theory as the heart of the American philosophy of government, not only for the revolutionary generation but for succeeding ones as well. Long after the particular grievances against George III have been forgotten, the belief that government exists to preserve the rights of the people, and can be dissolved if it fails to do so, remains a prime article of faith for Americans.

But even though the Declaration built upon generations of American and British experience, it went far beyond those ideas, and, in fact, as many modern writers have noted, it is a radical statement in its view of the purposes of government. As nation-states began emerging in Europe in the late middle ages, the common assumption had been that governments existed to ensure order and protect the stability of society. But the Declaration of Independence, while not denying the need for order, asserts that the prime purpose of government is to protect the rights of the individual. For the first time, it is the individual and not the society that is paramount, and the success of government is to be measured not by how well society is regulated, but by how free the individual is from government.

Jefferson's noble statement of the rights of mankind thus became a beacon for future generations, not only in the United States but throughout the world. One need not ignore the fact that Jefferson had to temporize, for American society in the eighteenth century did not treat all people equally. Native Americans, people without property, women and especially black slaves were considered neither equal nor endowed with rights. But the statement became the goal, the ideal, and it would be the standard against which future American society would be, and still is, judged.

The development of American democracy has been, in many ways, an elucidation of the premises outlined in the Declaration of Independence: that certain truths are self-evident, that people are created equal, that they are endowed with inalienable rights, that governments derive their power from the consent of the governed and that the purpose of government is to protect these rights. Such sentiments have not lost their power to inspire men and women to this day. They are the mark of the successes of American democracy, as well as of its failures.

Dual Federalism

One of the primary matters that the Founding Father's had to consider when they were writing the Constitution was how to design a government without giving any individual too much power. After the difficulties of freeing themselves from the British monarchy, they needed to ensure that it would never be the case on this continent.

For this reason the United States government was designed to have many layers of checks and balances. For example, the three branches of government. Another balancing system was a pattern of dual federalism. Dual federalism refers to government systems in which power is equally divided between two groups. This is exactly the type of system that was created by the separation of duties between the Federal government and the various State governments.

The Bill of Rights states that any power not specifically granted to the federal government in the Constitution remains the responsibility of the States. The dual federalism system has been altered with time. When the Great Depression prompted a series of social reform programs (collectively known as the New Deal) the federal government began to take superiority over the state governments. Up to this point, the federal government traditionally had little or no effect on the daily lives of individuals. These programs were federal programs that helped provide food, housing, work, and other necessities to individuals. The prominence of the federal government in daily life has continued and the dual federalism system has gradually faded with time.

Creating the Government

While the form of government adopted by the United States drew heavily on European sources, it was nonetheless distinctly American. The colonists, of course, brought English ideas with them when they crossed the Atlantic, but once here these ideas were slowly but definitely modified to reflect conditions in the New World.

The settlers, like their kin who stayed in England, believed that British government and the common law constituted the greatest protections of individual liberties that had ever existed. Magna Carta (1215) had laid down the great root principle of constitutional democracy, that a fundamental law exists beyond which no one, not even the king, may trespass. The rule of law, as it had developed in the centuries between Magna Carta and the first English settlement at Jamestown, came to encompass a parliament and a court system. The first to represent the interests of the people to their rulers, and the second to provide impartial administration of justice. Although the executive power and the symbols of majesty remained with the monarch, the parliament gradually won an important share of power through its control of taxes and the purse. The judicial system achieved its authority by mastery of the intricacies of the law.

The British system, both in theory and in practice, relied on the existence of an upper class, an aristocracy which had the wealth, leisure and education to devote to the problems of governing. In their studies of government, English writers posited a society of distinct classes and interests, all of which would be balanced so that no one part could dominate the others. It was in parliament that the various groups in society would be represented, look after their own interests, advance the greater interest of the realm and, above all, jealously guard the rights and properties of the people.

It is not surprising that the colonists tried to emulate these institutions when they created their own governments. Moreover, they took with them some powerful ideas then beginning to circulate in the Mother Country, such as the notion that the Puritans had developed of a compact or covenant. In the New England colonies especially, the covenant theory became an essential part of political as well as religious thought, expressing the idea that people covenanted with one another to form a government that they were bound to obey, provided it did not exceed the authority granted to it.

In the 169 years between the landing at Jamestown and the signing of the Declaration of Independence, the colonial experience diverged significantly from its English roots. Here there was no established aristocracy; no leisure class could devote itself to government. The settlers looked to those of their neighbors who had talents and abilities for leadership, with the result that the Americans came to see government less as the preserve of the upper classes than as an instrument for all the people. Because colonial society was so fluid, the notion of a parliament representing fixed interests made little sense; moreover, the towns and rural areas that sent representatives to their colonial legislatures gave them directions, often instructing them on how to vote on particular issues. While it is true that a majority of the settlers were disenfranchised because of gender, race or lack of property, the fact remains that popular participation in the political process was far greater in the colonies in the eighteenth century than in the Mother Country.

The Americans, even as they separated from the Crown, nonetheless claimed that all they wanted was their rights as Englishmen. After independence, as they set about creating union and government, they relied on two sources of thought: classic English political theory, and their own experiences. In the Articles of Confederation, the United States' first constitution, the framers relied more on theory, and aimed at creating a federal government that would avoid the problems associated with a strong central government, the very problem that had led to their revolt from Great Britain. But that system proved too weak for the task of governing the new nation, since it lacked sufficient powers. At the Philadelphia convention of 1787, John Dickinson, the chief author of the Articles, urged his fellow delegates: "Experience must be our only guide; reason may mislead us." The Constitution they drafted drew from both reason and experience, and as a result has proven a remarkably durable document.

But the Constitution, even after its adoption in 1788 and the addition of the first ten amendments, the Bill of Rights, in 1791, was little more than an outline of government. The Philadelphia convention had spelled out certain powers and limitations that it had considered important to have clearly articulated, but it left much of the actual operating structure to be worked out on the basis of experience. For example, there is no mention of a "cabinet" in the Constitution, yet George Washington, the first president, convened the heads of the executive departments on a regular basis to advise him, and the Cabinet has become part of the American government.

One unique aspect of the American system has been the role played by the courts. Although the Constitution set up three branches of government, the legislative, executive and judicial, it devoted relatively little space to the role of the courts, assuming that judges would know what to do. But unlike Great Britain, where there was little interplay between the courts and the other branches of government, in the United States the Supreme Court has become a balance wheel of constitutional government. The Supreme Court is the final arbiter of what the Constitution means. In many of its decisions in the last two centuries the Court has arbitrated between the executive and legislative branches, and has also spelled out both the powers and the limits of the federal government.

In the documents in this section, we see the beginnings of the American governmental system, and how it evolved into the basic constitutional scheme under which Americans still live.

American Society

There was an exuberance to be found in the United States of the early nineteenth century, a feeling of confidence in the ability of the new nation and of its people to overcome all difficulties. The Puritan dream of America as a "city upon a hill" seemed on the verge of becoming reality.

There were several sources for this optimism. The country, except during the War of 1812, was at peace, and that battle with England had seemed to many Americans the final act of the War for Revolution, confirming the new nation's independence. Despite some economic problems, the United States enjoyed great prosperity, with the opening of western lands making more than enough room for the newcomers from Europe seeking political freedom and opportunity. The purchase of Louisiana from France in 1803 extended American boundaries to the Pacific, and the Lewis and Clark expedition to explore the purchase reported that even more fertile lands and great forests lay awaiting exploration and settlement.

But the most important factor was the continued success of the national experiment in democracy. In the bloodless "revolution of 1800," as the election of 1800 came to be called, power had peacefully changed hands from the Federalists to the Republicans, an event then unparalleled in human history. Although slavery cast a shadow on the future (see Part IV), most Americans took pride in the fact that no other people in the world at that time enjoyed so much freedom. Despite the fears of the Anti-Federalists in the 1780s, the national government in Washington did nothing to invade the rights and privileges of its citizens. People joined enthusiastically in the political process, a fact noted with amazement by European visitors. If the ideal of the citizen as an engaged, conscientious member of the polity would take hold any place, it seemed that the new United States offered the most fertile soil.

This confidence did not preclude an awareness of problems, of the sense that Americans had not yet achieved a perfect society. But writers, artists and politicians all believed that these issues could be resolved, that the new Americans would be able to control their destiny and, to match the more perfect Union established by the Constitution, that they would create a more perfect society as well.

In this section we see this exuberance and confidence in a variety of documents that, with one exception, look forward to a more democratic society in which individual opportunity would be unfettered.

Crisis of the Union

In 1619 a ship put in at Jamestown, and sold twenty Negroes it had brought over from Africa as part of its cargo. Bound labor was common in all the colonies because of the intense labor shortage. Many settlers earned their passage to the New World, and that of their families, by indenturing themselves for a term of years, usually seven, after which they would be free. At least some of the early Africans were treated as indentured servants, because there are records of free blacks in the Chesapeake area in the 1650s. But about that time the white colonists determined that blacks would be slaves durante vita (for the term of their lives), and their children would be slaves as well.

Slaves became the backbone of the southern plantation system. The southern colonies relied on certain cash crops such as tobacco, rice and indigo, all of which were labor intensive, and slavery provided the least expensive and most reliable source of labor. At the time of the American Revolution, there were about 500,000 slaves in the thirteen colonies, out of a total population of roughly three million.

By then slavery, which had never been as extensive in the northern colonies, had begun to die out. Slavery did not make economic sense in the northern economies, and many northerners objected to the forced bondage of human beings. Some white southerners also looked forward to the end of slavery, and in fact much of the early abolitionist sentiment could be found in the South, not in the North. The invention of the cotton gin in the early nineteenth century made cotton an extremely profitable crop, however, and slavery continued to grow. By 1860 there were nearly four million black men and women in bondage.

At the Second Continental Congress there had been some discussion about slavery. How, after all, could the Congress declare that "All men are created equal" when Americans kept some men and women as slaves? But the agenda before the Congress was independence of the colonies from Great Britain, not the emancipation of slaves, and the northern delegates agreed to mute their concerns about slavery in order to achieve a united front against the king.

Similarly, at the Constitutional Convention in 1787, the delegates had come to Philadelphia to design a new system of government and not to abolish bondage. Slavery played practically no role in the debate, and those sections of the Constitution dealing with slaves (who are never identified as such), such as taxation, importation and counting for purposes of state representation, were quickly negotiated.

One reason slavery remained a mute issue was because in the eighteenth century human bondage was fairly widespread. Even though serfdom had disappeared from most of Europe, the notion of enslaving humans had roots going back many centuries. The Bible mentioned slavery as widespread, and did not condemn the practice. The Enlightenment writers ignored the issue, and the movement to abolish slavery did not take firm hold in England until the end of the eighteenth century.

Southerners moving westward took their slaves with them, and in 1819, when Missouri applied for entry into the Union, it did so as a slave state. In what struck many people, both North and South, as an amazing development, the House of Representatives refused admission, and instead passed a resolution calling on Missouri to end the practice. When Thomas Jefferson heard this news, he wrote to a friend that it struck him "as a firebell in the night," and he "considered it at once as the [death] knell of the Union."

Henry Clay managed to work out what came to be known as the Missouri Compromise, which permitted Missouri to enter the Union as a slave state but prohibited slavery in the rest of the immense Louisiana Purchase. But the issue would not go away, and within a relatively short time pressure began to build in the northern states to prevent the spread of slavery into the western territories, while some groups began agitating to end slavery in the United States altogether.

The southern states reacted angrily to this attack on what they termed their "peculiar institution." By the nineteenth century slavery served far more than demands for labor; bondage based on race had become essential to the southern caste system. It served as a tie between small farmers and the wealthy plantation owners, and as long as even poor whites could look down on black slaves, class differences could be glossed over.

As northern agitation increased, southerners argued that slavery was no one's business except their own, and held up the banner of states' rights to deflect abolitionist demands. What went on within their own borders was the business of each individual state, and not of any other state or of the national government.

But southerners wanted additional territory in which to expand their cotton holdings, they wanted the federal government to secure Texas for settlement by slaveholders, and they wanted a strict fugitive slave law authorizing the federal government to help capture and return runaway slaves. And they claimed all this as their right under the Constitution.

The result was the gradual deterioration of the ties that bound the country together. As abolitionist sentiment increased in the North, secessionist demands rose in the South. By the late 1850s, the United States was, in Abraham Lincoln's phrase, a "house divided," and on the verge of collapse.

When the southern states seceded from the Union after Lincoln's election as president in 1860, many voices in the North urged that they be let go; the remaining nation would be better without them, since it would be free of the taint of human bondage. But Lincoln and many other northerners believed that the Union had to be preserved, and the Civil War began as an effort to keep the Union together.

But slavery, which had led to this crisis, could not be ignored, and eventually the war became not just a crusade to save the Union, but one to end the "peculiar institution" as well. For Lincoln at Gettysburg, as well as for soldiers in the field, the fight had become a struggle for democracy, and for a while the outcome of that struggle remained in doubt.

War, even for noble purposes, creates strains upon a democratic society. Behavior that can be tolerated in peacetime, such as severe criticism of the government, is seen as threatening when the nation itself is at peril. The Civil War, fought for democracy and freedom, also had its dark side of intolerance and the invasion of civil liberties. In the end, the Union emerged stronger than before, with slavery abolished and democracy enthroned. As we shall see in subsequent sections, however, the issues were not fully resolved.

Industrial America

The United States underwent a period of enormous growth in the period between the Civil War and World War I. Between 1870 and 1900 alone, the population doubled from 38.6 million people to 76 million people. Much of this growth came from immigrants from Europe, and to make room for them, the country adopted the most liberal land policy in its history. America, which had been primarily a rural nation, was rapidly becoming urbanized, and the motor force behind all this change was the industrialization of the country's economy. In the same three decades that the population doubled, the nation's factories and mills quadrupled their output. Thanks to new technologies and new products, Americans lived better and lived longer, and even common workers came to enjoy the highest standard of living in the industrializing world.

But there was a price to be paid for all this progress. Factories polluted the air and water, and working conditions in mines and factories were frequently unsafe. The intimate labor relations of small stores and workshops gave way to the impersonalization of plants in which thousands of workers toiled twelve hours a day or more for bare subsistence wages.

What worried many Americans most, however, was the effect this new industrialization would have on the body politic. Prior to the Civil War, money played a relatively small part in national politics. (In fact, America had only one millionaire in this era, John Jacob Astor.) In towns and villages, and even in the small cities, local elites played a central role in political life, but politics at the state and national levels were truly democratic. What would happen if very rich individuals entered the political arena? How would the individual who wanted to participate in the nation's political life fare against such concentrations of wealth?

Reformers in this era worried constantly about the corruption of democracy, and sought a variety of measures to keep the political system not only honest, but open to everyone. Few of the reformers were anti-industry; there was no movement in the United States comparable to the Luddites in England. Nor were all of the reformers even anti-bigness, since many of them accepted as inevitable the growth of large industries.

But whatever their economic views, they shared the desire to keep the United States an open and democratic society, and as we see in this section, that commitment took a variety of forms.

Freedom of Expression

The First Amendment is considered by some to be the single most important guarantor of the rights of Americans, and the key to successful democratic government. The amendment protects several rights: freedom of religious practice, freedom from government-imposed religion, freedom of speech and the press, the right to assemble peacefully and the right to petition the government for redress.

These rights encompass all forms of expression, and the framers of the Constitution believed that in a democratic society, the right to express oneself without fear of government punishment was the basis of true and effective citizen participation in and control of the government. Thomas Jefferson believed that a free press, one that constantly monitored the activities of public officials, kept government from becoming tyrannical. Other commentators, from the eighteenth century on, picked up on this theme, and some of the most celebrated court cases in the nation's history have concerned the limits of free expression.

The colonists arrived in this country bringing with them English notions regarding the relation of church to society, as well as common law limits on speech and press. In England, and indeed in the rest of Europe, the notion of a single established church had been widespread for centuries. Both the ecclesiastical and the secular authorities were seen as agencies of God, with each supporting the other in carrying out their common duty. It made no more sense to have more than one religion in a society than to have more than one king; multiple religions, like multiple claimants to the crown, would do little but stir up antagonism.

When British settlers came to North America, they brought with them this idea of an established church, one which enjoyed a monopoly and the protection of the state, and which was supported by taxes imposed by the state. The Puritans who wished to escape what they saw as the corruption of the Church of England believed fervently in an established church, but of their own beliefs. In Virginia and a number of other colonies, the Anglican Church enjoyed the same status in the New World as it did in the Mother Country.

But in America, unlike England, a number of competing religions vied with the Anglican Church for the loyalty of the settlers. Dissident sects who were persecuted for their heresies in the British Isles and on the continent came to the American colonies, where they preached their doctrines and gained adherents. By the time of the American Revolution, no one faith, even in colonies with established churches, really commanded the loyalty of a large majority of the people. But because there were so many groups, Americans necessarily learned to tolerate dissenting viewpoints.

Similarly, freedom of speech and press also underwent a transformation in the colonies. In England the law of libel had been very clear: if you printed a statement that attacked a person's reputation or impugned the integrity of a government official, you were guilty of libel, regardless of the truth or falsity of the statement. The libel trial of John Peter Zenger in 1734 made the first significant American modification to this rule. Zenger, accused of seditious libel, appealed to the jury to determine not just the fact that he had printed statements regarding the governor's conduct, but whether they were true; if true, he claimed, then he should not be held liable for having printed them. Zenger won, and now the truth of the statement could be entered as a complete defense to the charge of libel, a rule not adopted in the mother country until the nineteenth century.

But the notion of seditious libel, of statements impugning the authority of government, remained part of American law even beyond the adoption of the First Amendment. In 1798 the government passed the Sedition Law, which fully embodied English views, and in World War I the Sedition Act was passed to limit criticism of the government. Beginning with the war case of Abrams v. United States in 1919, the judiciary began to move away from the older British notions, and to adopt the modern American view that free and unhindered speech, no matter how offensive it may be to the government or to others, is to be the rule, and that there can be no government censorship of ideas.

Prior restraint is a practice of forbidding the publishing of certain materials before they have been published. The US Supreme Court has ruled the practice of prior restraint to be one of the most serious violations of the first amendment (which protects the freedom of speech). Prior restraint will occasionally be required by a judge, but the circumstances have to be very compelling. Typically, prior restraint is used in high profile cases in which the judge believes that publishing certain information will have the effect of potentially harming an ongoing case. If a judge has strong reason to believe that the partiality of the jury will be lost if the information begins to circulate, then the judge may issue prior restraint. However, in all other cases it is considered a violation of the law.

The development of First Amendment rights is not complete. Contemporary social passions, varieties of religious beliefs and the strong feeling among many that religion ought to be supported by government, the built-in conflict between a press that wants to know everything and governments that wish to disclose as little as possible as well as the implications of modern technology for retrieving and disseminating information continue to make the debate over the meaning and limits of the First Amendment timely and of eternal importance to democratic society.

Facing the World

When the first European settlers came to New England, they deliberately set out to create a new and more moral society than the one they had left behind. This new society was to be "a city upon a hill," and a beacon to all mankind. Arrogant as that theme may sound, it has been a constant refrain through much of American history. The men who signed the Declaration of Independence saw their rebellion not as a simple matter of wanting to exchange one form of government for another, but of standing up, in the sight of the world, for certain immutable principles of liberty and democracy. A little over a dozen years later, many of these same men cheered the French Revolution as a candle lit by their own flame. And in the midst of a great civil war, Abraham Lincoln called the American form of government "mankind's last, best hope."

There are some who see American diplomacy as little more than blending together democratic idealism and a realistic concern for national interest. The American goals of liberty, democracy and free enterprise are, in their eyes, most worthy goals which other nations ought to be encouraged to emulate. American wars, in this mindset, have been fought for noble purposes. And there is no question but that Americans have been most comfortable when foreign policy has led to war if they could honestly believe that they were fighting for justice and democratic ideals.

A second school of thought, shared by laypersons and scholars alike, labels itself as more realistic. This group believes that too often in its past, the United States has been naive in its foreign policy, and because they do enjoy a democratic society, Americans tend to oscillate between a policy of isolation designed to insulate the country from evil foreign influences and meaningless foreign wars, and a policy of militant internationalism designed to make other nations over into their own image.

The truth is somewhere in between, but probably closer to the "realist" point of view. There is no question but that a more hardheaded analysis of American interests might have led to less belligerency and less involvement in some overseas adventures. But it is also true that American ideals are not simple abstractions, but do in fact play a key role in determining American policy.

The United States was blessed for well over a century after gaining its independence by its ability to avoid entangling itself in foreign affairs. Given the simple modes of transportation and communication available at the time, the Atlantic and Pacific oceans served as great natural barriers to insulate the country from the rest of the world. This is just what the founding generation wanted, and at least in part the purchase of the great Louisiana territory from France in 1803 was designed to give Americans sufficient room to expand for generations. When European nations lost additional colonies in the

New World, the United States was strong enough to tell them that the Americas were no longer subject to European designs.

But the world changed, and the United States, slowly and reluctantly, had to change as well. Against its wishes, the nation was drawn into two world wars and then, as can be seen in Part IX, it became entangled in a forty-year Cold War as well. Whether one wishes to consider it naivete or not, the articulation of American foreign policy aims in terms of ideals was important, not only to the people at home, but to nations and their citizens overseas. Just as the Declaration of Independence took on meanings far beyond what its drafters may have intended, so Wilson's vision of a world order as articulated in the Fourteen Points, Franklin Roosevelt's notion of mutual security and the Atlantic Charter and Jimmy Carter's belief in the need for international decency also took on meanings that far transcended their immediate purpose.

Cynics may complain that these high-sounding phrases meant little, that all they did was to cover up base motives of imperialism and expansionism. But words are important, and statements such as these regarding foreign policy help to define a nation's character as much as do noble declarations of internal policies.

Cold War Issues

The joy that accompanied the defeat of Germany and Japan in 1945 quickly turned to consternation as America's wartime ally, the Soviet Union, suddenly became its enemy in what would be a forty-year-long Cold War.

The Cold War put great strains on American society and government. It required the nation to reassess certain priorities and assumptions, a process not always easy to accomplish. Americans are used to thinking of foreign policy matters in black-or-white terms: a nation is our friend or enemy, a policy is good or bad, a war can be won or lost. Harry Truman devised what would be the heart of American foreign policy for the Cold War, a policy known as containment. Its goal was to ensure that the Soviet Union did not expand further than eastern Europe, and when the communist forces pushed, the United States would push back, but only with measured force.

The war allowed Americans to be generous, as they showed in the Marshall Plan, but the Cold War also led to some serious strains upon the body politic. In the midst of a war, an unpopular president had to fire a popular general in order to reassert civilian control over the military. The Supreme Court had to declare a presidential action taken under the war powers as unconstitutional, something not done since the Civil War. And the ugly side of democracy, the face of the mob, made a brief but fearsome appearance in the form of McCarthyism. But the nation survived the Cold War, and in doing so actually strengthened a number of democratic principles.

A More Inclusive America

The motto of the United States, E pluribus unum, means "out of many, one." From the beginning, many different peoples have come to the United States, and most of them quickly acculturated into American society. As early as 1790 the first census of the new nation revealed that in Virginia, the most "English" of states, three out of ten people were of German origin. On the American landscape numerous ethnic groups could be counted, and a name such as O'Brien was as common in Boston as in Dublin. Words, foods and customs from other countries all found their way into the American culture, enriching it over the centuries. Oscar Handlin, the noted historian, began his classic study of immigration, The Uprooted (1951), with the following observation: "Once I thought to write a history of the immigrants in America. Then I discovered that the immigrants were American history."

Not all immigrants came willingly, and descendants of the enslaved Africans brought to the New World in chains have just recently begun to demand full acceptance into society. Moreover, the old notion that immigrants and their children had to shed their "alien" customs to become "real" Americans has recently given way to ethnic pride and the idea that both the society and the ethnic group are enriched through pride in origin and some retention of the "old ways."

But the process of inclusion has not always been smooth. Throughout American history there were periods of intense nativism, in which those whose families had been in the United States three or four generations attempted to keep out newcomers, or the majority Protestants discriminated against Catholics and Jews, or Anglo-Saxons kept Orientals in an inferior position. The gates of America, which had been wide open in the nineteenth century, began to close early in the twentieth, although in the last few decades a more liberal policy of accepting those fleeing persecution or seeking new opportunity has been established.

Inclusion, however, applies not only to immigrants. As American society has become more open and democratic, groups that traditionally had been assigned an inferior place in society began demanding equal rights and full acceptance. Women, gays and lesbians, Latinos, African Americans, Native Americans and others called for an expansion of the democratic ideal to include them as well. "Multiculturalism" has become an important and hotly debated concept in modern America, with its advocates demanding that all sources of culture be given credit for their contributions, not just those that derived from western Europe.

At times these debates have been shrill, even ugly, but they have contributed to the democratic nature of American society. They are also uniquely American, because no other nation on Earth has prided itself as the United States has on its ethnic and cultural diversity.

Civil Liberties

Civil liberties are protections from negative government actions. They are basic rights and freedoms derived from the Bill of Rights, the Constitution, or rights that have been accepted by courts and lawmakers throughout the years. The best examples of this are our First Amendment rights. For example, citizens are guaranteed the right to practice the religion of their choice. Therefore, the government cannot interfere in peoples religious worship because the 1st Amendment gives them "liberty" from the government.

Civil rights refer to the basic right to be free from unequal treatment. This involves positive actions the government should take to create equality. The term "civil rights" is associated with the protection of minority groups discriminated against based on race, gender, or disability. Civil rights protects in instances such as equal opportunity employment and housing. For example, as an employee, Sarah is not guaranteed the right to a promotion, but as a female employee she cannot legally be denied the promotion based on her gender. If this occurs, the employer has engaged in unlawful employment discrimination, which is a violation of Sarah's civil rights.

Continuing Vitality

In April 1975, the anniversary of the Revolutionary battles of Concord and Lexington, the United States began celebrating its bicentennial, a series of events that stretched out to cover the 200th anniversaries of the Declaration of Independence, the Constitution, the Judiciary Act and the Bill of Rights, as well as several other intermediary happenings. While many aspects of this prolonged national birthday party were, expectedly, celebratory in nature, there was also a significant amount of introspection. What was unique about the American system? Why had it worked so well? What were its most significant successes, and its most abject failures? Would an eighteenth-century document be able to guide the United States into the twenty-first century?

Scholars and laypersons alike disagreed on the answers to many of these questions, but in general they did conclude that the American experiment of an open, pluralist and democratic society had shown a resilience that allowed it to overcome crises few of the Founding Fathers could have anticipated. They did not claim that the system was perfect, but rather, that as certain problems have been overcome and more groups admitted into society as equal partners, the democratic system has shown an amazingly strong sense of continuing vitality. If it can continue to meet challenges in the future as it has in the past, then one can hope that American democracy, with all its flaws, will continue to provide, as Thomas Jefferson believed it would, man's best hope for governing himself.

What is Democracy?

Democracy may be a word familiar to most, but it is a concept still misunderstood and misused in a time when totalitarian regimes and military dictatorships alike have attempted to claim popular support by pinning democratic labels upon themselves. Yet the power of the democratic idea has also evoked some of history's most profound and moving expressions of human will and intellect: from Pericles in ancient Athens to Vaclav Havel in the modern Czech Republic, from Thomas Jefferson's Declaration of Independence in 1776 to Andrei Sakharov's last speeches in 1989.

In the dictionary definition, democracy "is government by the people in which the supreme power is vested in the people and exercised directly by them or by their elected agents under a free electoral system." In the phrase of Abraham Lincoln, democracy is a government "of the people, by the people, and for the people."

Freedom and democracy are often used interchangeably, but the two are not synonymous. Democracy is indeed a set of ideas and principles about freedom, but it also consists of a set of practices and procedures that have been molded through a long, often tortuous history. In short, democracy is the institutionalization of freedom. For this reason, it is possible to identify the time-tested fundamentals of constitutional government, human rights, and equality before the law that any society must possess to be properly called democratic.

Democracies fall into two basic categories, direct and representative. In a direct democracy, all citizens, without the intermediary of elected or appointed officials, can participate in making public decisions. Such a system is clearly only practical with relatively small numbers of people in a community organization or tribal council, for example, or the local unit of a labor union, where members can meet in a single room to discuss issues and arrive at decisions by consensus or majority vote. Ancient Athens, the world's first democracy, managed to practice direct democracy with an assembly that may have numbered as many as 5,000 to 6,000 persons, perhaps the maximum number that can physically gather in one place and practice direct democracy.

Modern society, with its size and complexity, offers few opportunities for direct democracy. Even in the northeastern United States, where the New England town meeting is a hallowed tradition, most communities have grown too large for all the residents to gather in a single location and vote directly on issues that affect their lives.

Today, the most common form of democracy, whether for a town of 50,000 or nations of 50 million, is representative democracy, in which citizens elect officials to make political decisions, formulate laws, and administer programs for the public good. In the name of the people, such officials can deliberate on complex public issues in a thoughtful and systematic manner that requires an investment of time and energy that is often impractical for the vast majority of private citizens.

How such officials are elected can vary enormously. On the national level, for example, legislators can be chosen from districts that each elect a single representative. Alternatively, under a system of proportional representation, each political party is represented in the legislature according to its percentage of the total vote nationwide. Provincial and local elections can mirror these national models, or choose their representatives more informally through group consensus instead of elections. Whatever the method used, public officials in a representative democracy hold office in the name of the people and remain accountable to the people for their actions.

Majority Rule and Minority Rights

All democracies are systems in which citizens freely make political decisions by majority rule. But rule by the majority is not necessarily democratic: No one, for example, would call a system fair or just that permitted 51 percent of the population to oppress the remaining 49 percent in the name of the majority. In a democratic society, majority rule must be coupled with guarantees of individual human rights that, in turn, serve to protect the rights of minorities, whether ethnic, religious, or political, or simply the losers in the debate over a piece of controversial legislation. The rights of minorities do not depend upon the goodwill of the majority and cannot be eliminated by majority vote. The rights of minorities are protected because democratic laws and institutions protect the rights of all citizens.

Diane Ravitch, scholar, author, and a former assistant U.S. secretary of education, wrote in a paper for an educational seminar in Poland: "When a representative democracy operates in accordance with a constitution that limits the powers of the government and guarantees fundamental rights to all citizens, this form of government is a constitutional democracy. In such a society, the majority rules, and the rights of minorities are protected by law and through the institutionalization of law."

These elements define the fundamental elements of all modern democracies, no matter how varied in history, culture, and economy. Despite their enormous differences as nations and societies, the essential elements of constitutional government, majority rule coupled with individual and minority rights, and the rule of law, can be found in Canada and Costa Rica, France and Botswana, Japan and India.

Democratic Society

Democracy is more than a set of constitutional rules and procedures that determine how a government functions. In a democracy, government is only one element coexisting in a social fabric of many and varied institutions, political parties, organizations, and associations. This diversity is called pluralism, and it assumes that the many organized groups and institutions in a democratic society do not depend upon government for their existence, legitimacy, or authority.

Thousands of private organizations operate in a democratic society, some local, some national. Many of them serve a mediating role between individuals and the complex social and governmental institutions of which they are a part, filling roles not given to the government and offering individuals opportunities to exercise their rights and responsibilities as citizens of a democracy.

These groups represent the interests of their members in a variety of ways: by supporting candidates for public office, debating issues, and trying to influence policy decisions. Through such groups, individuals have an avenue for meaningful participation both in government and in their own communities. The examples are many and varied: charitable organizations and churches, environmental and neighborhood groups, business associations and labor unions.

In an authoritarian society, virtually all such organizations would be controlled, licensed, watched, or otherwise accountable to the government. In a democracy, the powers of the government are, by law, clearly defined and sharply limited. As a result, private organizations are free of government control; on the contrary, many of them lobby the government and seek to hold it accountable for its actions. Other groups, concerned with the arts, the practice of religious faith, scholarly research, or other interests, may choose to have little or no contact with the government at all.

In this busy private realm of democratic society, citizens can explore the possibilities of freedom and the responsibilities of self-government - unpressured by the potentially heavy hand of the state.

The Pillars of Democracy

- Sovereignty of the people.
- Government based upon consent of the governed.
- Majority rule.
- Minority rights.
- Guarantee of basic human rights.
- Free and fair elections.
- Equality before the law.
- Due process of law.
- Constitutional limits on government.
- Social, economic, and political pluralism.
- Values of tolerance, pragmatism, cooperation, and compromise.

Equality and the Law

The right to equality before the law, or equal protection of the law as it is often phrased, is fundamental to any just and democratic society. Whether rich or poor, ethnic majority or religious minority, political ally of the state or opponent, all are entitled to equal protection before the law.

The democratic state cannot guarantee that life will treat everyone equally, and it has no responsibility to do so. However, writes constitutional law expert John P. Frank, "Under no circumstances should the state impose additional inequalities; it should be required to deal evenly and equally with all of its people."

No one is above the law, which is, after all, the creation of the people, not something imposed upon them. The citizens of a democracy submit to the law because they recognize that, however indirectly, they are submitting to themselves as makers of the law. When laws are established by the people who then have to obey them, both law and democracy are served.

Due Process

In every society throughout history, Frank points out, those who administer the criminal justice system hold power with the potential for abuse and tyranny. In the name of the state, individuals have been imprisoned, had their property seized, and been tortured, exiled and executed without legal justification and often without any formal charges ever being brought. No democratic society can tolerate such abuses.

Every state must have the power to maintain order and punish criminal acts, but the rules and procedures by which the state enforces its laws must be public and explicit, not secret, arbitrary, or subject to political manipulation by the state.

What are the essential requirements of due process of law in a democracy?

No one's home can be broken into and searched by the police without a court order showing that there is good cause for such a search. The midnight knock of the secret police has no place in a democracy.

No person shall be held under arrest without explicit, written charges that specify the alleged violation. Not only are persons entitled to know the exact nature of the charge against them, they also must be released immediately, under the doctrine known as habeas corpus, if the court finds that the charge is without justification or the arrest is invalid.

Persons charged with crimes should not be held for protracted periods in prison. They are entitled to a speedy and public trial, and to confront and question their accusers.

The authorities are required to grant bail, or conditional release, to the accused pending trial if there is little likelihood that the suspect will flee or commit other crimes. "Cruel and unusual" punishment, as determined by the traditions and laws of the society, is prohibited.

Persons cannot be compelled to be witnesses against themselves. This prohibition against involuntary self- incrimination must be absolute. As a corollary, the police may not use torture or physical or psychological abuse against suspects under any circumstances. A legal system that bans forced confessions immediately reduces the incentives of the police to use torture, threats, or other forms of abuse to obtain information, since the court will not allow such information to be placed into evidence at the time of trial.

Persons shall not be subject to double jeopardy; that is, they cannot be charged with the same crime twice. Any person tried by a court and found not guilty can never be charged with that same crime again.

Because of their potential for abuse by the authorities, so-called ex post facto laws are also proscribed. These are laws made after the fact so that someone can be charged with a crime even though the act was not illegal at the time it occurred.

Defendants may possess additional protections against coercive acts by the state. In the United States, for example, the accused have a right to a lawyer who represents them in all stages of a criminal proceeding, even if they cannot pay for such legal representation themselves. The police must also inform suspects of their rights at the time of their arrest, including the right to an attorney and the right to remain silent (to avoid self- incrimination).

A common tactic of tyranny is to charge opponents of the government with treason. For this reason, the crime of treason must be carefully limited in definition so that it cannot be used as a weapon to stifle criticism of the government.
None of these restrictions means that the state lacks the necessary power to enforce the law and punish offenders. On the contrary, the criminal justice system in a democratic society will be effective to the degree that its administration is judged by the population to be fair and protective of individual rights, as well as of the public interest.

Judges may be either appointed or elected to office, and hold office for specified terms or for life. However they are chosen, it is vital that they be independent of the nation's political authority to ensure their impartiality. Judges cannot be removed for trivial or merely political reasons, but only for serious crimes or misdeeds and then only through a formal procedure, such as impeachment (the bringing of charges) and trial in the legislature.

The rock upon which a democratic government rests is its constitution. The formal statement of its fundamental obligations, limitations, procedures, and institutions. The constitution of the country is the supreme law of the land, and all citizens, prime ministers to peasants alike, are subject to its provisions. At a minimum, the constitution, which is usually codified in a single written document, establishes the authority of the national government, provides guarantees for fundamental human rights, and sets forth the government's basic operating procedures.

Despite their enduring, monumental qualities, constitutions must be capable of change and adaptation if they are to be more than admirable fossils. The world's oldest written constitution, that of the United States, consists of seven brief articles and 27 amendments. This written document, however, is only the foundation for a vast structure of judicial decisions, statutes, presidential actions, and traditional practices that has been erected over the past 200 years and kept the U.S. Constitution alive and relevant.

This pattern of constitutional evolution takes place in every democracy. In general, there are two schools of thought about the process of amending, or changing, a nation's constitution. One is to adopt a difficult procedure, requiring many steps and large majorities. As a result, the constitution is changed infrequently, and then only for compelling reasons that receive substantial public support. This is the model of the United States, whose Constitution is a brief statement of the general principles, powers, and limits of government, together with a more specific listing of duties, procedures, and, in the Bill of Rights, the fundamental rights of individual citizens.

A much simpler method of amendment, which many nations use, is to provide that any amendment may be adopted by approval of the legislature and passed by the voters at the next election. Constitutions able to be changed in this fashion can be quite lengthy, with specific provisions that differ little from the general body of legislation.

No constitution like America's, written in the 18th century, could have survived unchanged into the late 20th century. Similarly, no constitution in force today will survive into the next century without the capacity for change, while still holding fast to principles of individual rights, due process, and government through the consent of the governed.

The Three Branches: Legislative

The Legislative branch of the government consists of the bicameral Congress, which was formed thanks to the Connecticut Compromise. Congress, as a whole body, has some specific responsibilities:

- Making laws
- Setting rules related to naturalization
- Dealing with commerce
- Establishing post offices
- Declaring war

The Congress is not in session all year. In fact, their sessions usually last from the beginning of January until the end of July. The session can be extended, if necessary.

House of Representatives

The House of Representatives does not have a fixed number of members, because the number of representatives each state has is determined by its population. Currently, there are 435 members. The number of Representatives per state is determined through the Census which takes place every 10 years. If a state's population has increased or decreased, its number of representatives is reapportioned.

Representatives are elected every two years through direct elections held in their states. They are elected so often because their role is to represent the current needs and interests of the people, so if those needs and interests change the people may want to elect different Representatives.

Each state divides itself into districts, and each district selects a different representative. The idea behind districting is that it allows the entire state to be represented. For example, without districting, all of California's 52 representatives might have been from the southern end of the state so they would not have understood the concerns of the northern part of the state. With districting, each section of the state is fairly represented.

Districting, however, has not been without its problems. One of the most common was gerrymandering, or the creation of districts with the intention of giving one political party an advantage. The Reapportionment Act which was passed in 1929 set restrictions on the practice of gerrymandering.

To run for the office, a person must meet specific qualifications that are outlined in Article I of the Constitution:

- must be at least 25 years old
- must live in the state he or she wants to represent
- must have been a citizen of the United States for at least 7 years

The House of Representatives has two specific responsibilities:

1. Creating bills related to taxation
2. Determining whether a government official should be put on trial if he or she commits a crime against the United States. This process is known as impeachment.

The Senate

The Senate contains a fixed number of members because each state is given an equal number of seats – two – in this part of Congress, regardless of their population. Therefore, there are currently 100 Senators.

Senators are elected every six years. Originally, the Constitution called for Senators to be selected by a state's legislature, but this was changed with the passing of Amendment XVII. Now, Senators – like Representatives – are chosen through direct elections.

The term of a Senator is more lengthy than that of a Representative because a Senator's job is to represent the needs and interests of the people over the long term. He or she is supposed to consider the "big picture."

To run for the office, a person must meet specific qualifications that are outlined in Article I of the Constitution:

- must be at least 30 years old
- must live in the state he or she wants to represent
- must have been a citizen of the United States for at least 9 years

The Senate has several specific responsibilities:

1. Holding impeachment trials
2. Approving treaties
3. Approving presidential appointments to seats on the Supreme Court, in cabinets, and as ambassadors

Cloture is a procedure that allows the Senate to place a time limit on the consideration of a bill or other matter. The goal of cloture is to stop attempts to block or delay Senate action on a matter. When a bill is being discussed, some parties prolong the discussion of the bill as a tactic. They can do this by offering numerous procedural motions, by debating it at length, or by other obstructive actions. Under the cloture rule, the Senate may limit consideration of a pending matter to 30 additional hours. To obtain cloture, a vote of three-fifths of the full Senate is necessary.

Speaker of the House

The speaker of the house is the most important member in the House of Representatives. Not only is he or she third in line for the Presidency through succession, but is also in an important leadership position.

The Speaker is nominated and elected by a straight-party vote of the entire House. The Speaker has many rights and powers which include:

- Placing peers in specific committees
- Head the House of Representatives
- Set the House's agenda
- Interpret rules of action

Majority and Minority Leaders

The majority leader is the second or principle deputy to the Speaker of the House. This person is elected by a secret ballot at the beginning of the Congressional term. The person in this job is the "right hand man" of the speaker and helps him or her with whatever assistance they require including logistics, etc.

The minority leader is the leader of the party of opposition in the House. For example, if the Speaker of the House is Republican, the minority leader will be a Democrat. The minority leader will work with both the Speaker and the majority leader to organize debates, agendas and other matters.

Whips

Whips are deputies who hold an administrative position in each of the two main parties. Their function is to tally votes and rally party loyalty towards supporting the party position. The majority and minority whips also have deputy whips that help with this function. A basic understanding is that these whips are individuals meant to keep the members in line.

Congress

Congress is made up of both the House and the Senate.

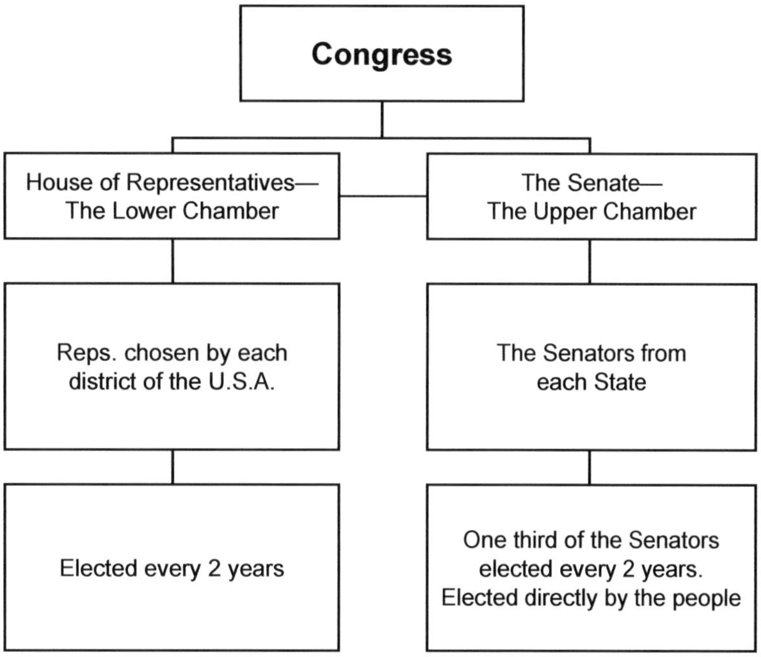

The broad powers of the whole Congress are spelled out in Article I of the Constitution:

- To levy and collect taxes;
- To borrow money for the public treasury;
- To make rules and regulations governing commerce among the states and with foreign countries;
- To make uniform rules for the naturalization of foreign citizens;
- To coin money, state its value, and provide for the punishment of counterfeiters;
- To set the standards for weights and measures;
- To establish bankruptcy laws for the country as a whole;
- To establish post offices and post roads;
- To issue patents and copyrights;
- To set up a system of federal courts;
- To punish piracy;
- To declare war;
- To raise and support armies;
- To provide for a navy;
- To call out the militia to enforce federal laws, suppress lawlessness, or repel invasions;
- To make all laws for the seat of government (Washington, D.C.);
- To make all laws necessary to enforce the Constitution.

A few of these powers are now outdated, but they remain in effect. The Tenth Amendment sets definite limits on congressional authority, by providing that powers not delegated to the national government are reserved to the states or to the people. In addition, the Constitution specifically forbids certain acts by Congress. It may not:

- Suspend the writ of habeas corpus – a requirement that those accused of crimes be brought before a judge or court before being imprisoned – unless necessary in time of rebellion or invasion;
- Pass laws that condemn persons for crimes or unlawful acts without a trial;
- Pass any law that retroactively makes a specific act a crime;
- Levy direct taxes on citizens, except on the basis of a census already taken;
- Tax exports from any one state;
- Give specially favorable treatment in commerce or taxation to the seaports of any state or to the vessels using them;
- Authorize any titles of nobility.

Officers of the Congress

The Constitution provides that the vice president shall be president of the Senate. The vice president has no vote, except in the case of a tie. The Senate chooses a president *pro tempore* to preside when the vice president is absent. The House of Representatives chooses its own presiding officer - the Speaker of the House. The speaker and the president pro tempore are always members of the political party with the largest representation in each house.

At the beginning of each new Congress, members of the political parties select floor leaders and other officials to manage the flow of proposed legislation. These officials, along with the presiding officers and committee chairpersons, exercise strong influence over the making of laws.

How a Bill Becomes a Law

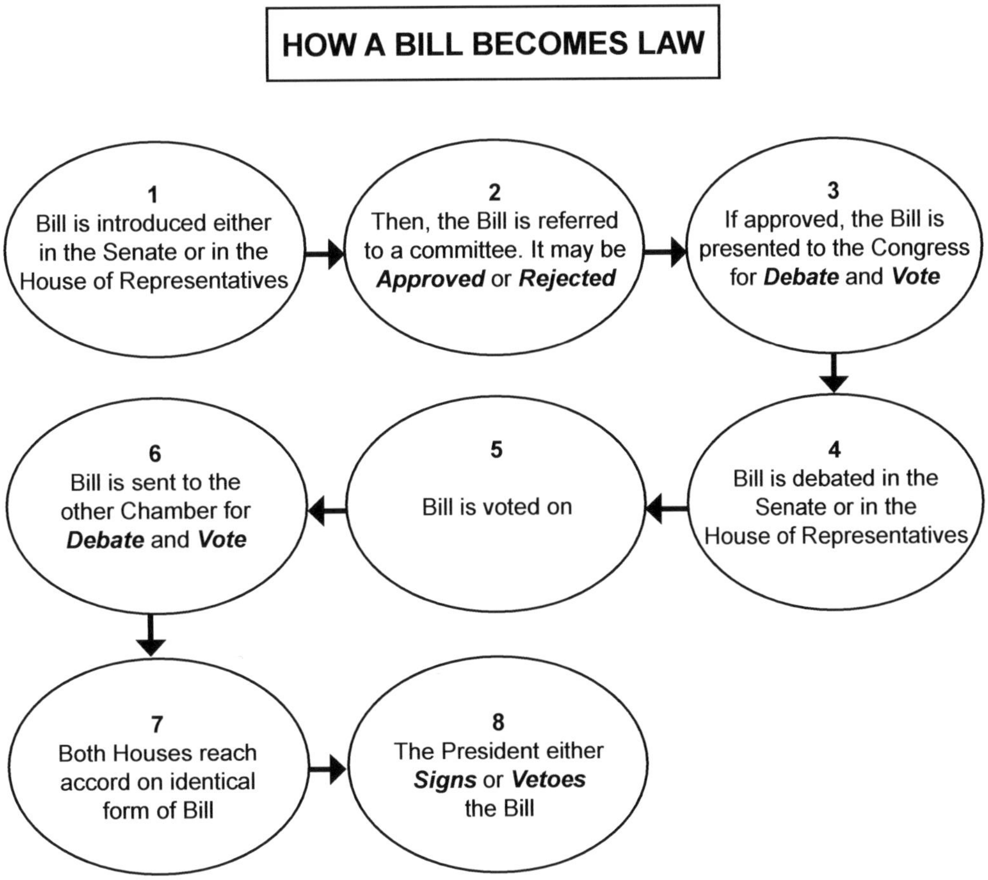

The Committee Process

One of the major characteristics of the Congress is the dominant role committees play in its proceedings. Committees have assumed their present-day importance by evolution, not by constitutional design, since the Constitution makes no provision for their establishment.

At present the Senate has 17 standing (or permanent) committees; the House of Representatives has 19 committees. Each specializes in specific areas of legislation: foreign affairs, defense, banking, agriculture, commerce, appropriations, and other fields. Almost every bill introduced in either house is referred to a committee for study and recommendation. The committee may approve, revise, kill, or ignore any measure referred to it. It is nearly impossible for a bill to reach the House or Senate floor without first winning committee approval. In the House, a petition to release a bill from a committee to the floor requires the signatures of 218 members; in the Senate, a majority of all members is required. In practice, such discharge motions only rarely receive the required support.

The majority party in each house controls the committee process. Committee chairpersons are selected by a caucus of party members or specially designated groups of members. Minority parties are proportionally represented on the committees according to their strength in each house.

Bills are introduced by a variety of methods. Some are drawn up by standing committees; some by special committees created to deal with specific legislative issues; and some may be suggested by the president or other executive officers. Citizens and organizations outside the Congress may suggest legislation to members, and individual members themselves may initiate bills. After introduction, bills are sent to designated committees that, in most cases, schedule a series of public hearings to permit presentation of views by persons who support or oppose the legislation. The hearing process, which can last several weeks or months, opens the legislative process to public participation.

One virtue of the committee system is that it permits members of Congress and their staffs to amass a considerable degree of expertise in various legislative fields. In the early days of the republic, when the population was small and the duties of the federal government were narrowly defined, such expertise was not as important. Each representative was a generalist and dealt knowledgeably with all fields of interest. The complexity of national life today calls for special knowledge, which means that elected representatives often acquire expertise in one or two areas of public policy.

When a committee has acted favorably on a bill, the proposed legislation is then sent to the floor for open debate. In the Senate, the rules permit virtually unlimited debate. In the House, because of the large number of members, the Rules Committee usually sets limits. When debate is ended, members vote either to approve the bill, defeat it, table it – which means setting it aside and is tantamount to defeat – or return it to committee. A bill passed by one house is sent to the other for action. If the bill is amended by the second house, a conference committee composed of members of both houses attempts to reconcile the differences.

Once passed by both houses, the bill is sent to the president, for constitutionally the president must act on a bill for it to become law. The president has the option of signing the bill – by which it becomes law – or vetoing it. A bill vetoed by the president must be reapproved by a two-thirds vote of both houses to become law.

The president may also refuse either to sign or veto a bill. In that case, the bill becomes law without his signature 10 days after it reaches him (not counting Sundays). The single exception to this rule is when Congress adjourns after sending a bill to the president and before the 10-day period has expired; his refusal to take any action then negates the bill – a process known as the "pocket veto."

Congressional Powers of Investigation

One of the most important nonlegislative functions of the Congress is the power to investigate. This power is usually delegated to committees – either to the standing committees, to special committees set up for a specific purpose, or to joint committees composed of members of both houses. Investigations are conducted to gather information on the need for future legislation, to test the effectiveness of laws already passed, to inquire into the qualifications and performance of members and officials of the other branches, and, on rare occasions, to lay the groundwork for impeachment proceedings. Frequently, committees call on outside experts to assist in conducting investigative hearings and to make detailed studies of issues.

There are important corollaries to the investigative power. One is the power to publicize investigations and their results. Most committee hearings are open to the public and are widely reported in the mass media. Congressional investigations thus represent one important tool available to lawmakers to inform the citizenry and arouse public interest in national issues. Congressional committees also have the power to compel testimony from unwilling witnesses and to cite for contempt of Congress witnesses who refuse to testify and for perjury those who give false testimony.

Informal Practices of Congress

In contrast to European parliamentary systems, the selection and behavior of U.S. legislators has little to do with central party discipline. Each of the major American political parties is a coalition of local and state organizations that join together as a national party – Republican or Democratic – during the presidential elections at four-year intervals. Thus the members of Congress owe their positions to their local or state electorate, not to the national party leadership nor to their congressional colleagues. As a result, the legislative behavior of representatives and senators tends to be individualistic and idiosyncratic, reflecting the great variety of electorates represented and the freedom that comes from having built a loyal personal constituency.

Congress is thus a collegial and not a hierarchical body. Power does not flow from the top down, as in a corporation, but in practically every direction. There is only minimal centralized authority, since the power to punish or reward is slight. Congressional policies are made by shifting coalitions that may vary from issue to issue. Sometimes, where there are conflicting pressures – from the White House and from important economic or ethnic groups – legislators will use the rules of procedure to delay a decision so as to avoid alienating an influential sector. A matter may be postponed on the grounds that the relevant committee held insufficient public hearings. Or Congress may direct an agency to prepare a detailed report before an issue is considered. Or a measure may be put aside ("tabled") by either house, thus effectively defeating it without rendering a judgment on its substance.

There are informal or unwritten norms of behavior that often determine the assignments and influence of a particular member. "Insiders," representatives and senators who concentrate on their legislative duties, may be more powerful within the halls of Congress than "outsiders," who gain recognition by speaking out on national issues. Members are expected to show courtesy toward their colleagues and to avoid personal attacks, no matter how unpalatable their opponents' policies may be. Members are also expected to specialize in a few policy areas rather than claim expertise in the whole range of legislative concerns. Those who conform to these informal rules are more likely to be appointed to prestigious committees or at least to committees that affect the interests of a significant portion of their constituents.

The most powerful and coveted positions are on the Appropriations, Rules, and Ways and Means committees. In general, each House member serves on two committees, except for Appropriations, Rules, and Ways and Means committees. The least popular committees include House Administration and Standards of Official Conduct.

Standing, or Permanent, Committees of Congress

STANDING, OR PERMANENT, COMMITTEES OF CONGRESS	
House of Representatives	Senate
Agriculture	Agriculture, Nutrition, and Forestry
Appropriations	Appropriations
Armed Services	Armed Services
Banking and Financial Services	Banking
Budget	Budget
Commerce	Commerce, Science, and Transportation
Education and the Workforce	Energy and Natural Resources
Government Reform and Oversight	Environment and Public Works
House Administration	Finance
International Relations	Foreign Relations
Judiciary	Governmental Affairs
Resources	Health, Education, Labor, and Pension
Rules	Indian Affairs
Science	Judiciary
Small Business	Rules and Administration
Standards of Official Conduct	Small Business
Transportation and Infrastructure	Veterans' Affairs
Veterans' Affairs	
Ways and Means	

Oversight Powers of Congress

Dictionaries define "oversight" as "watchful care," and this approach has proven to be one of the most effective techniques that Congress has adopted to influence the executive branch. Congressional oversight prevents waste and fraud; protects civil liberties and individual rights; ensures executive compliance with the law; gathers information for making laws and educating the public; and evaluates executive performance. It applies to cabinet departments, executive agencies, regulatory commissions, and the presidency.

Congress's oversight function takes many forms:

- Committee inquiries and hearings;
- Formal consultations with and reports from the president;
- Senate advice and consent for presidential nominations and for treaties;
- House impeachment proceedings and subsequent Senate trials;
- House and Senate proceedings under the Twenty-fifth Amendment in the event that the president becomes disabled, or the office of the vice president falls vacant;
- Informal meetings between legislators and executive officials;
- Congressional membership on governmental commissions;
- Studies by congressional committees and support agencies such as the Congressional Budget Office, the General Accounting Office, and the Office of Technology Assessment – all arms of Congress.

The oversight power of Congress has helped to force officials out of office, change policies, and provide new statutory controls over the executive. In 1949, for example, probes by special Senate investigating subcommittees revealed corruption among high officials in the Truman administration. This resulted in the reorganization of certain agencies and the formation of a special White House commission to study corruption in the government.

The Senate Foreign Relations Committee's televised hearings in the late 1960s helped to mobilize opposition to the Vietnam War. Congress's 1973 Watergate investigation exposed White House officials who illegally used their positions for political advantage, and the House Judiciary Committee's impeachment proceedings against President Richard Nixon the following year ended his presidency. Select committee inquiries in 1975 and 1976 identified serious abuses by intelligence agencies and initiated new legislation to control certain intelligence activities.

In 1983, congressional inquiry into a proposal to consolidate border inspection operations of the U.S. Customs Service and the U.S. Immigration and Naturalization Service raised questions about the executive's authority to make such a change without new legislation. In 1987, oversight efforts disclosed statutory violations in the executive branch's secret arms sales to Iran and the diversion of arms profits to anti-government forces in Nicaragua, known as the contras. Congressional findings resulted in proposed legislation to prevent similar occurrences.

Investigation by a bipartisan congressional commission and subsequent Senate hearings in 1996 and 1997 uncovered instances of abuse and mismanagement in the Internal Revenue Service (IRS), the federal agency responsible for collecting income tax payments. The Senate Finance Committee heard testimony from IRS agents who claimed that the pressure on them to recover unpaid taxes was so great that taxpayers were sometimes harassed and from citizens who said they were wrongly accused and aggressively pursued by the IRS for failure to pay taxes. In 1998, the Congress passed IRS reform legislation that created an independent oversight board and expanded taxpayers' protections, which included shifting the burden of proof in tax disputes from the taxpayer to the IRS.

Time and again, the oversight power of Congress has proven to be an essential check in monitoring the presidency and controlling public policy.

War Powers Act

The pattern of checks and balances was implemented into the government to ensure a distribution of power. However, with time, gray areas in the system have been noted and exploited by various branches of the government.

One such gray area is the process of engaging in warfare. The Constitution clearly awards Congress the right of making declarations of war on other countries. However, the President is named Commander-In-Chief of the armed forces. As a result of this apparent dual-responsibility there is often conflict between the executive and legislative branches of government in determining the proper time to enter conflict.

When President Nixon engaged in the long and taxing Vietnam War without the approval of Congress, Congress quickly passed the War Powers Act in an attempt to prevent future administrations from doing the same thing. The purpose of the Act is to require collaboration between Congress and the President any time warfare is imminent. It requires that no military conflict can continue longer than 60 days unless Congress approves it and issues a declaration of war. Otherwise, troops must be promptly pulled out of conflict after 60 days.

President Nixon vetoed the Act, but it passed despite his efforts. However, there still continues to be a fair amount gray space in military conflicts as most Presidents seek to find loopholes around following the provisions of the Act - either by withdrawing from conflict before the required 60 days, arguing the unconstitutionality of the requirement, or claiming that their acts don't truly qualify as warfare.

A Country of Many Governments

The federal entity created by the Constitution is the dominant feature of the American governmental system. But the system itself is in reality a mosaic, composed of thousands of smaller units – building blocks that together make up the whole. There are 50 state governments plus the government of the District of Columbia, and further down the ladder are still smaller units that govern counties, cities, towns, and villages.

This multiplicity of governmental units is best understood in terms of the evolution of the United States. The federal system, it has been seen, was the last step in an evolutionary process. Prior to the Constitution, there were the governments of the separate colonies (later states) and, prior to those, the governments of counties and smaller units. One of the first tasks accomplished by the early English settlers was the creation of governmental units for the tiny settlements they established along the Atlantic coast. Even before the Pilgrims disembarked from their ship in 1620, they formulated the Mayflower Compact, the first written American constitution. And as the new nation pushed westward, each frontier outpost created its own government to manage its affairs.

The drafters of the U.S. Constitution left this multilayered governmental system untouched. While they made the national structure supreme, they wisely recognized the need for a series of governments more directly in contact with the people and more keenly attuned to their needs. Thus, certain functions – such as defense, currency regulation, and foreign relations – could only be managed by a strong centralized government. But others – such as sanitation, education, and local transportation – could be better served by local jurisdictions.

STATE GOVERNMENT

Before their independence, colonies were governed separately by the British Crown. In the early years of the republic, prior to the adoption of the Constitution, each state was virtually an autonomous unit. The delegates to the Constitutional Convention sought a stronger, more viable federal union, but they were also intent on safeguarding the rights of the states.

In general, matters that lie entirely within state borders are the exclusive concern of state governments. These include internal communications; regulations relating to property, industry, business, and public utilities; the state criminal code; and working conditions within the state. Within this context, the federal government requires that state governments must be democratic in form and that they adopt no laws that contradict or violate the federal Constitution or the laws and treaties of the United States.

There are, of course, many areas of overlap between state and federal jurisdictions. Particularly in recent years, the federal government has assumed ever broadening responsibility in such matters as health, education, welfare, transportation, and housing and urban development. But where the federal government exercises such responsibility in the states, programs are usually adopted on the basis of cooperation between the two levels of government, rather than as an imposition from above.

Like the national government, state governments have three branches: executive, legislative, and judicial; these are roughly equivalent in function and scope to their national counterparts. The chief executive of a state is the governor, elected by popular vote, typically for a four-year term (although in a few states the term is two years). Except for Nebraska, which has a single legislative body, all states have a bicameral legislature, with the upper house usually called the Senate and the lower house called the House of Representatives, the House of Delegates, or the General Assembly. In most states, senators serve four-year terms, and members of the lower house serve two-year terms.

The constitutions of the various states differ in some details but generally follow a pattern similar to that of the federal Constitution, including a statement of the rights of the people and a plan for organizing the government. On such matters as the operation of businesses, banks, public utilities, and charitable institutions, state constitutions are often more detailed and explicit than the federal one. Each state constitution, however, provides that the final authority belongs to the people, and sets certain standards and principles as the foundation of government.

CITY GOVERNMENT

Once predominantly rural, the United States is today a highly urbanized country, and about 80 percent of its citizens now live in towns, large cities, or suburbs of cities. This statistic makes city governments critically important in the overall pattern of American government. To a greater extent than on the federal or state level, the city directly serves the needs of the people, providing everything from police and fire protection to sanitary codes, health regulations, education, public transportation, and housing.

The business of running America's major cities is enormously complex. In terms of population alone, New York City is larger than 41 of the 50 states. It is often said that, next to the presidency, the most difficult executive position in the country is that of mayor of New York.

City governments are chartered by states, and their charters detail the objectives and powers of the municipal government. But in many respects the cities function independently of the states. For most big cities, however, cooperation with both state and federal organizations is essential to meeting the needs of their residents.

Types of city governments vary widely across the nation. However, almost all have some kind of central council, elected by the voters, and an executive officer, assisted by various department heads, to manage the city's affairs.

There are three general types of city government: the mayor-council, the commission, and the city manager. These are the pure forms; many cities have developed a combination of two or three of them.

Mayor-Council. This is the oldest form of city government in the United States and, until the beginning of the 20th century, was used by nearly all American cities. Its structure is similar to that of the state and national governments, with an elected mayor as chief of the executive branch and an elected council that represents the various neighborhoods forming the legislative branch. The mayor appoints heads of city departments and other officials, sometimes with the approval of the council. He or she has the power of veto over ordinances (the laws of the city) and frequently is responsible for preparing the city's budget. The council passes city ordinances, sets the tax rate on property, and apportions money among the various city departments.

The Commission. This combines both the legislative and executive functions in one group of officials, usually three or more in number, elected city-wide. Each commissioner supervises the work of one or more city departments. One is named chairperson of the body and is often called the mayor, although his or her power is equivalent to that of the other commissioners.

The City Manager. The city manager is a response to the increasing complexity of urban problems, which require management expertise not often possessed by elected public officials. The answer has been to entrust most of the executive powers, including law enforcement and provision of services, to a highly trained and experienced professional city manager.

The city manager plan has been adopted by a growing number of cities. Under this plan, a small, elected council makes the city ordinances and sets policy, but hires a paid administrator, also called a city manager, to carry out its decisions. The manager draws up the city budget and supervises most of the departments. Usually, there is no set term; the manager serves as long as the council is satisfied with his or her work.

COUNTY GOVERNMENT

The county is a subdivision of the state, usually containing two or more townships and several villages. New York City is so large that it is divided into five separate boroughs, each a county in its own right: the Bronx, Manhattan, Brooklyn, Queens, and Staten Island. On the other hand, Arlington County, Virginia, just across the Potomac River from Washington, D.C., is both an urbanized and suburban area, governed by a unitary county administration.

In most U.S. counties, one town or city is designated as the county seat, and this is where the government offices are located and where the board of commissioners or supervisors meets. In small counties, boards are chosen by the county as a whole; in the larger ones, supervisors represent separate districts or townships. The board levies taxes; borrows and appropriates money; fixes the salaries of county employees; supervises elections; builds and maintains highways and bridges; and administers national, state, and county welfare programs.

TOWN AND VILLAGE GOVERNMENT

Thousands of municipal jurisdictions are too small to qualify as city governments. These are chartered as towns and villages and deal with such strictly local needs as paving and lighting the streets; ensuring a water supply; providing police and fire protection; establishing local health regulations; arranging for garbage, sewage, and other waste disposal; collecting local taxes to support governmental operations; and, in cooperation with the state and county, directly administering the local school system.

The government is usually entrusted to an elected board or council, which may be known by a variety of names: town or village council, board of selectmen, board of supervisors, board of commissioners. The board may have a chairperson or president who functions as chief executive officer, or there may be an elected mayor. Governmental employees may include a clerk, treasurer, police and fire officers, and health and welfare officers.

One unique aspect of local government, found mostly in the New England region of the United States, is the "town meeting." Once a year – sometimes more often if needed – the registered voters of the town meet in open session to elect officers, debate local issues, and pass laws for operating the government. As a body, they decide on road construction and repair, construction of public buildings and facilities, tax rates, and the town budget. The town meeting, which has existed for more than two centuries, is often cited as the purest form of direct democracy, in which the governmental power is not delegated, but is exercised directly and regularly by all the people.

OTHER LOCAL GOVERNMENTS

The federal, state, and local governments covered here by no means include the whole spectrum of American governmental units. The U.S. Bureau of the Census (part of the Commerce Department) has identified no less than 84,955 local governmental units in the United States, including counties, municipalities, townships, school districts, and special districts.

Americans have come to rely on their governments to perform a wide variety of tasks which, in the early days of the republic, people did for themselves. In colonial days, there were few police officers or firefighters, even in the large cities; governments provided neither street lights nor street cleaners. To a large extent, people protected their own property and saw to their families' needs.

Now, meeting these needs is seen as the responsibility of the whole community, acting through government. Even in small towns, the police, fire, welfare, and health department functions are exercised by governments. Hence, the bewildering array of jurisdictions.

HOW TO MAKE AMENDMENTS TO THE CONSTITUTION

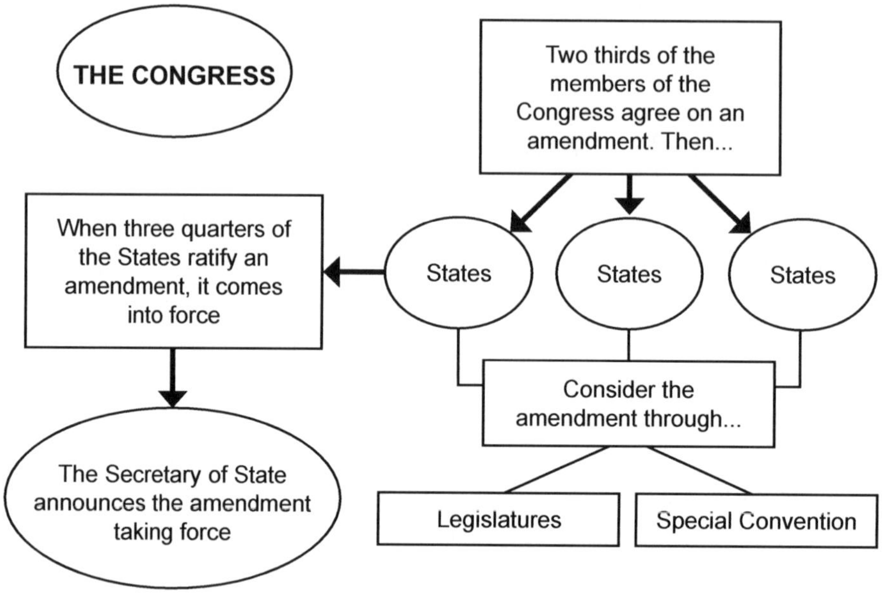

The Supreme Court also interprets the constitution the way it deems fit and just. The first ever judicial review came in 1803 in the case of Marbury vs. Madison in which the Supreme Court declared an act of the Congress unconstitutional.

The Three Branches: Executive

The head of the Executive branch of the government is the President. The President is not the only member of the Executive branch. This branch also includes the vice president and the cabinet members.

The President

The authors of the Constitution realized that someone was needed to serve as the head of state in order, but they were concerned that such a person may end up wielding too much power and thus becoming no better than a monarch. The system of checks and balances they developed, however, keeps that from occurring.

The President is elected every four years. Unlike Representatives and Senators who are directly elected by their constituents, the President is elected indirectly through the Electoral College, which was established by Article II of the Constitution.

To run for the office, a person must meet specific qualifications that are outlined in Article I of the Constitution:

- must be at least 35 years old
- must have lived in the United States for at least 14 years
- must be a natural-born citizen of the United States

While members of Congress can be re-elected repeatedly, the President can only run for two terms. This was not always the case. Franklin Roosevelt ran four times for the office and won each time. Six years after his death, Amendment XXII was passed to limit the number of terms a president can have.

The President has specific powers which are granted to him under the Constitution:

1. Creating treaties
2. Making appointments to the Supreme Court and to the cabinets
3. Vetoing bills passed by Congress
4. Calling special sessions of Congress
5. Being commander-and-chief of the armed forces (allows the President to use military action without the approval of the Senate)
6. Acting as a diplomat

The Constitution gives the President the power to veto bills that Congress presents to him. If he vetoes the bill, Congress is given the chance to override his veto by a two-thirds vote. Any bill that the President neglects to sign or to veto after ten days (not including Sundays) becomes a law as if he had signed it. If Congress adjourns in the interim, the bill dies. The process starts over and the bill must be presented again before it can be voted on again. Andrew Jackson referred to this as the "Pocket Veto."

In the general sense, a mandate is an order or authorization to complete a task. When this term is applied to the Presidential Mandate it is an indication that a candidate has received the support of the people and is obligated to uphold the promises he made while campaigning. Essentially the Presidential Mandate is the responsibility that the new President has to fulfill the promises he made to voters. A President is said to have a mandate from the people when he has received a significant majority of the votes in an election. This indicates that the vast majority of the country is in support of his political agenda.

The Vice-President

The Vice-President is basically the second-in-command. He assumes control of the Executive Branch when the President is unable to do so, particularly as a result of death or impeachment.

The Vice-President is elected every four years along with the President. When the Constitution was first written, there was no separate election for vice-president. Instead, the role was given to the candidate for president who received the second highest number of votes. With the development of political parties, this system caused a number of problems.

These problems escalated during the 1800 election when Thomas Jefferson and Aaron Burr received the same number of votes. Burr was intended to be Jefferson's running mate since they came from the same party, but since they received the same number of votes from Electors in the Electoral College, it wasn't clear which one would be named President.

The matter went to the House of Representatives which finally decided that Jefferson would be president and Burr would be his vice-president. As a result of the election, a new amendment was passed in 1804 (Amendment XII) which required a separate vote for the president and the vice-president.

The Vice-Presidential candidate must meet the same requirements as far as age and citizenship as the Presidential candidate. In addition, the Constitution states that if both candidates are from the same state the electors in that state are not allowed to cast their votes for both. As a result, the vice-presidential candidate could end up not getting enough electoral votes to win the office. Therefore, most vice-presidential candidates come from different states than the presidential candidates.

Traditionally, presidential candidates select their own running mates. Their selections are considered final until that candidate has been officially nominated during the party's convention.

Besides his role as successor in the event the president is incapacitated, the vice-president also serves as the President of the Senate. If there is a tied vote in the Senate, the vice-president must cast the tie-breaking vote. Vice-presidents also have other roles that have not been specifically assigned by the Constitution. Generally, they provide advice and guidance to the president. They also speak out about the policies of the administration and often have "pet projects" that they want to work on. For example, Lyndon Johnson was in charge of the space program while he served as John F. Kennedy's vice-president.

The Cabinet

Within the Executive Branch are also fifteen separate departments that deal with specific issues, such as education and defense. Each of these departments has one person as their leader, and these leaders are appointed by the president and their appointments must be approved by the Senate. These leaders are collectively referred to as the Cabinet.

After taking office, George Washington encouraged Congress to acknowledge the need for departments to handle many of the affairs of the country. During Washington's administration, there were only a handful of departments and their leaders were given the title Secretary. His cabinet consisted of the following positions:

- Attorney General
- Secretary of State
- Postmaster General
- Secretary of War
- Secretary of the Treasury

As the country grew, more departments have been added and the Cabinet has continued to grow. The most recently added department, Homeland Security, was created in 2003.

Below is a list of all of the departments, the dates they were created, and a brief description of their role in the government:

Department of State (1789) – The most notable job of the Secretary of State is to advise the president about foreign policies. The Secretary of State is the highest-ranking member of the Cabinet.

Department of the Treasury (1789) – This department handles economic matters, and its Secretary is the president's main economic advisor.

Department of the Interior (1849) – Generally, this office is mostly concerned with issues related to wildlife and national parks.

Department of Agriculture (1862) – This department provides a number of services, including providing advice to farmers and ensuring the safety of food produced in the United States.

Department of Justice (1870) – The Attorney General (the only cabinet member without the title of Secretary) provides the president with legal advice.

Department of Commerce (1903) – Business and industry issues are the primary focus of this department.

Department of Labor (1913) – This department and the Department of Commerce used to be united. Now, it is a separate department that focuses on issues related to workers in the United States.

Department of Defense (1947) – This department's main responsibility is overseeing all of the branches of the military.

Department of Health and Human Services (1953) – As the name implies, this department is concerned with health issues.

Department of Housing and Urban Development (1965) – The members of this department are in charge of helping to develop communities.

Department of Transportation (1966) – This department is in charge of overseeing all methods of transportation, including air travel, highways, and railroads.

Department of Energy (1977) – The primary concern of this department is regulating and producing energy for use in the United States.

Department of Education (1979) – This department develops guidelines for American education and deals with issues related to education. Until 1979, these issues were handled by the Department of Health, Education, and Welfare.

Department of Veterans' Affairs (1988) – This department maintains and develops programs to help veterans and their families.

Department of Homeland Security (2003) – This department is concerned with preventing and/or protecting the country from terrorist attacks.

There are no specific qualifications that one must possess to be part of the Cabinet, except that Cabinet members cannot have any other legislative or judicial positions. Cabinet members are often former political figures. Many have been Senators, Representatives, and governors before their appointments. In more recent years, it has become common for non-political figures, such as businesspeople, to be selected for these positions.

While the Cabinet plays an important role in the formation of U.S. policies, its members are not given authority equal to that of the President. He oversees all of their activities.

The Three Branches: Judicial

The final branch of the government interprets the laws made by Congress and works to uphold the Constitution. Only the Supreme Court is thoroughly discussed in Article III of the Constitution, but Congress is given the right to create additional courts and to determine their appropriate jurisdiction.

The Judicial branch is primarily concerned with protecting the rights of the individual as outlined in the Constitution. In order to do this, two sets of courts have been established: State Courts and Federal Courts. The Supreme Court, which is the highest court in the country, is part of the Federal Court system.

State Courts

Most legal cases are heard in state courts, particularly the Superior Courts which are known as the main courts of original jurisdiction (because they hear the case first). Superior Courts can hear both criminal and civil cases.

When a case is decided in the Superior Court, but the losing party is not satisfied with the decision, the course can be taken to the next level of state courts: the State Appellate Court. When a case is appealed in these courts, no jury is used. Instead, a number of judges listen to the case and decide whether the decision should be overturned, the decision was correct, or a new trial should be held.

If the losing party's appeal does not succeed, he or she can take the case to the highest level of state court: the State's Supreme Court. The decision of the state's Supreme Court is final.

Judges for all of the state courts are usually elected through direct elections. Depending on the court, judges serve terms of between 4-12 years.

Federal Courts

While state courts deal with a wide range of cases, including divorce, murder, and embezzlement, federal courts are given jurisdiction over only specific crimes, such as bank robbery and counterfeiting, and civil matters, such as environmental issues. There are three levels of Federal courts also.

The lowest level is the District courts which serve particular sections of the United States. The District Courts have original jurisdiction over all federal cases. Additionally, cases at the state level which deal with constitutional disputes are also heard first in District courts.

Cases decided at the District level can be brought before the Court of Appeals for the possibility of overturning the decision or holding a new trial. At least two judges must be present to hear the appeals case and their decisions are considered final unless the Supreme Court, which is the highest Federal court, agrees to hear them.

All Federal judges are appointed by the president and are allowed to serve for life unless they resign or are impeached.

Solicitor General

The Solicitor General is an officer of the U.S. Justice Department. He or she represents the federal government in cases before the U.S. Supreme Court. The United States is involved as a plaintiff in the majority of cases the U.S. Supreme Court decides on. The federal government litigates thousands of cases each year. The Solicitor General is aided by staff attorneys, Deputy Solicitors General and Assistants to the Solicitor General. Another responsibility of the Solicitor General is to review any cases decided in the lower courts to determine whether they should be appealed and what position should be taken. A large percent of petitions for Writ of Certiorari that are granted are made by the Solicitor General.

The Supreme Court

The Supreme Court is the highest court in the country. It's made up of eight justices and one Chief Justice. Justices are appointed to their positions by the president with the approval of the Senate. Because justices, like other federal judges, serve until death, retirement, or impeachment, these appointments are extremely important.

While the Supreme Court is asked to revisit an average of 7500 cases every year, they generally review less than 100 of them. The cases heard by the Supreme Court and their decisions regarding those cases can have long-term effects for society. For example, the Supreme Court's 1954 decision to desegregate schools in Brown v. Board of Education of Topeka led to the eventual desegregation of schools all across the United States. Despite the Court's important ruling, however, some school systems remained segregated up until 1970. The Executive and Legislative branches would have been responsible for ensuring the schools took the appropriate steps following the decision, since the Court can only interpret the law, not enforce it.

Twice a week, the justices convene to go over cases that could possibly be reviewed. For a case to be selected for review, four of the justices must agree to hear it. If a case is not selected, then the decision handed down by the lower courts is deemed to be final.

After hearing a case, the Supreme Court justices have a conference to determine their decisions. Each justice writes down his or her decision about the case and the vote is recorded. Only five votes are needed to finalize a decision.

Once the decision is reached, it is written out by the justices along with the reasons used for reaching that decision. Justices who do not agree with the majority can write a dissenting opinion which is recorded.

As explained above, the Supreme Court is important because its decisions have widespread effects not just for the individuals involved in the cases it reviews but every citizen of the United States. Because the law is not clearly spelled out, the justices have to determine how laws apply to different situations, as well as what the authors of the Constitution intended for some of the passages to mean.

Writ of Certiorari

When a person is not satisfied with the ruling on a case, they may petition the Supreme Court to review the decision. A petition for Writ of Certiorari is a request that the Supreme Court order a lower court to send up the record of a case for review. It lists the parties, the facts of the case, the legal questions presented for review, and arguments why the Court should grant the petition. The Court isn't obligated to hear the case, and can grant or deny the petition. Usually, the Court only reviews cases of national significance or cases with precedent. Only a handful of the cases that are petitioned are granted Writ of Certiorari.

Supreme Court Cases

1803 – Marbury v. Madison – Often called the most important decision in the history of the Supreme Court, Marbury v. Madison established the principle of judicial review and the power of the Court to determine the constitutionality of legislative and executive acts.

The case arose from a political dispute in the aftermath of the presidential election of 1800 in which Thomas Jefferson, a Democratic-Republican, defeated the incumbent president, John Adams, a Federalist. In the closing days of Adams's administration, the Federalist-dominated Congress created a number of judicial positions, including 42 justices of the peace for the District of Columbia. The Senate confirmed the appointments, the president signed them, and it was the responsibility of the secretary of state to seal the commissions and deliver them. In the rush of last-minute activities, the outgoing secretary of state failed to deliver commissions to four justices of the peace, including William Marbury.

The new secretary of state under President Jefferson, James Madison, refused to deliver the commissions because the new administration was angry that the Federalists had tried to entrench members of their party in the judiciary. Marbury brought suit in the Supreme Court to order Madison to deliver his commission.

If the Court sided with Marbury, Madison might still have refused to deliver the commission, and the Court had no way to enforce the order. If the Court ruled against Marbury, it risked surrendering judicial power to the Jeffersonians by allowing them to deny Marbury the office he was legally entitled to. Chief Justice John Marshall resolved this dilemma by ruling that the Supreme Court did not have authority to act in this case. Marshall stated that Section 13 of the Judiciary Act, which gave the Court that power, was unconstitutional because it enlarged the Court's original jurisdiction from the jurisdiction defined by the Constitution itself. By deciding not to decide in this case, the Supreme Court secured its position as the final arbiter of the law.

1824 – Gibbons B. Ogden – The first government of the United States under the Articles of Confederation was weak partly because it lacked the power to regulate the new nation's economy, including the flow of interstate commerce. The Constitution gave the U.S. Congress the power "to regulate commerce...among the several states....," but that authority was challenged frequently by states that wanted to retain control over economic matters.

In the early 1800s, the state of New York passed a law that required steamboat operators who traveled between New York and New Jersey to obtain a license from New York. Aaron Ogden possessed such a license; Thomas Gibbons did not. When Ogden learned that Gibbons was competing with him, and without permission from New York, Ogden sued to stop Gibbons.

Gibbons held a federal license to navigate coastal waters under the Coasting Act of 1793, but the New York State courts agreed with Ogden that Gibbons had violated the law because he did not have a New York State license. When Gibbons took his case to the Supreme Court, however, the justices struck down the New York law as unconstitutional because it infringed on the U.S. Congress's power to regulate commerce. "The word 'to regulate' implies, in its nature, full power over the thing to be regulated," the Court said. Therefore, "it excludes, necessarily, the action of all others that would perform the same operation on the same thing."

1856 – Dred Scott v. Sanford – Dred Scott was a slave whose owner, John Emerson, took him from Missouri, a state that allowed slavery, to Illinois, where slavery was prohibited. Several years later Scott returned to Missouri with Emerson. Scott believed that because he had lived in a free state, he should no longer be considered a slave.

Emerson died in 1843, and three years later Scott sued Emerson's widow for his freedom. Scott won his case in a Missouri court in 1850, but in 1852 the state supreme court reversed the lower court's decision. Meanwhile, Mrs. Emerson remarried, and Scott became the legal property of her brother, John Sanford (misspelled as Sandford in court records). Scott sued Sanford for his freedom in federal court, and the court ruled against Scott in 1854.

When the case went to the Supreme Court, the justices ruled that Scott did not become a free man by virtue of having lived in a free state and that, as a black man, Scott was not a citizen and therefore was not entitled to bring suit in a court of law. The decision was widely criticized, and it contributed to the election of Abraham Lincoln, who opposed slavery, as president in 1860 and hastened the start of the Civil War in 1861. Dred Scott v. Sandford was overturned by the Thirteenth Amendment to the Constitution, which abolished slavery in 1865, and the Fourteenth Amendment, which granted citizenship to former slaves in 1868.

1893 – Nix v. Hedden – Determined that a tomato was classified as a vegetable, not a fruit.

1896 – Plessy v. Ferguson – Supported the idea of "separate but equal" in relation to segregation.

1919 – Schenck v. United States – Limited the right of freedom of speech by stating that those rights did not apply to speech which created a "clear and present danger."

1925 – Pierce v. Society of Sisters of the Holy Names of Jesus and Mary – Recognized that individuals have a right to privacy.

1937 – National Labor Relations Board (NLRB) V. Jones & Laughlin Steel Corp. – While Gibbons v. Ogden established the supremacy of Congress in regulating interstate commerce, NLRB v. Jones & Laughlin extended congressional authority from regulation of commerce itself to regulation of the business practices of industries that engage in interstate commerce.

Jones & Laughlin, one of the nation's largest steel producers, violated the National Labor Relations Act of 1935 by firing 10 employees for engaging in union activities. The act prohibited a variety of unfair labor practices and protected the rights of workers to form unions and to bargain collectively. The company refused to comply with an NLRB order to reinstate the workers. A Circuit Court of Appeals declined to enforce the board's order, and the Supreme Court reviewed the case.

At issue in this case was whether or not Congress had the authority to regulate the "local" activities of companies engaged in interstate commerce – that is, activities that take place within one state. Jones & Laughlin maintained that conditions in its factory did not affect interstate commerce and therefore were not under Congress's power to regulate. The Supreme Court disagreed, stating that "the stoppage of those [manufacturing] operations by industrial strife would have a most serious effect upon interstate commerce.... Experience has abundantly demonstrated that the recognition of the right of employees to self-organization and to have representatives of their own choosing for the purpose of collective bargaining is often an essential condition of industrial peace." By upholding the constitutionality of the National Labor Relations Act, the Supreme Court handed a victory to organized labor and set the stage for more far-reaching regulation of industry by the federal government.

1954 – Brown v. Board of Education of Topeka – Prior to this historic case, many states and the District of Columbia operated racially segregated school systems under the authority of the Supreme Court's 1896 decision in Plessy v. Ferguson, which allowed segregation if facilities were equal. In 1951 Oliver Brown of Topeka, Kansas, challenged this "separate-but-equal" doctrine when he sued the city school board on behalf of his eight-year-old daughter. Brown wanted his daughter to attend the white school that was five blocks from their home, rather than the black school that was 21 blocks away. Finding the schools substantially equal, a federal court ruled against Brown.

Meanwhile, parents of other black children in South Carolina, Virginia, and Delaware filed similar lawsuits. Delaware's court found the black schools to be inferior to white schools and ordered black children to be transferred to white schools, but school officials appealed the decision to the Supreme Court.

The Court heard arguments from all these cases at the same time. The briefs filed by the black litigants included data and testimony from psychologists and social scientists who explained why they thought segregation was harmful to black children. In 1954 a unanimous Supreme Court found that "...in the field of education the doctrine of 'separate but equal' has no place," and ruled that segregation in public schools denies black children "the equal protection of the laws guaranteed in the Fourteenth Amendment."

1957 – Roth v. United States – Determined that obscene material is not protected by the First Amendment

1961 – Torcaso v. Watkins – Explained that the government can not force a person to hold specific religious beliefs

1962 – Baker v. Carr – Determined that reapportioning Congressional districts must be done in order to preserve the idea of "one man, one vote"

1964 – New York Times Co. V. Sullivan – The First Amendment to the U.S. Constitution guarantees freedom of the press, but for years the Supreme Court refused to use the First Amendment to protect the media from libel lawsuits – lawsuits based on the publication of false information that damages a person's reputation. The Supreme Court's ruling in New York Times Co. v. Sullivan revolutionized libel law in the United States by deciding that public officials could not sue successfully for libel simply by proving that published information is false. The Court ruled that the complainant also must prove that reporters or editors acted with "actual malice" and published information "with reckless disregard of whether it was false or not."

The case arose from a full-page advertisement placed in the New York Times by the Southern Christian Leadership Conference to raise money for the legal defense of civil rights leader Martin Luther King, Jr., who had been arrested in Alabama in 1960. L.B. Sullivan, a city commissioner in Montgomery, Alabama, who was responsible for the police department, claimed that the ad libeled him by falsely describing the actions of the city police force. Sullivan sued the four clergymen who placed the ad and the New York Times, which had not checked the accuracy of the ad.

The advertisement did contain several inaccuracies, and a jury awarded Sullivan $500,000. The Times and the civil rights leaders appealed that decision to the Supreme Court, and the Court ruled unanimously in their favor. The Court decided that libel laws cannot be used "to impose sanctions upon expression critical of the official conduct of public officials," and that requiring critics to guarantee the accuracy of their remarks would lead to self-censorship. The Court found no evidence that the Times or the clergymen had malicious intent in publishing the ad.

1966 – Miranda v. Arizona – Clarence Earl Gideon was arrested for breaking into a poolroom in Florida in 1961. When he requested a court-appointed lawyer to defend him, the judge denied his plea, saying that state law required appointment of a lawyer only in capital cases – cases involving a person's death or calling for the death penalty. Gideon defended himself and was found guilty. While in prison, he spent hours in the library studying law books and handwriting a petition to the Supreme Court to hear his case. The Court decided that Gideon was denied a fair trial and ruled that every state must provide counsel for people accused of crimes who cannot afford to hire their own. When Gideon was retried with the help of a defense attorney, he was acquitted.

Just three years later the Supreme Court decided that the accused should have the right to counsel long before they get to a courtroom. Ernesto Miranda was convicted in a state court in Arizona of kidnapping and rape. His conviction was based on a confession Miranda gave to police officers after two hours of questioning, without being advised that he had the right to have an attorney present. In its ruling the Supreme Court required that police officers, when making arrests, must give what are now known as Miranda warnings – that suspects have the right to remain silent, that anything they say may be used against them, that they can have a lawyer present during questioning, and that a lawyer will be provided if they cannot afford one.

Miranda v. Arizona is one of the Supreme Court's best known decisions, as Miranda warnings are dramatized routinely in American movies and television programs. However, in 1999 a federal court of appeals challenged the decision in the case of Dickerson v. United States, in which a convicted bank robber claimed he had not been properly read his rights. In June 2000, the Supreme Court overturned Dickerson in a 7-to-2 ruling that strongly reaffirmed the validity of Miranda.

1969 – Tinker v. Des Moines Independent Community School District – Protected the free speech rights of students and teachers in public schools.

1969 – Brandenburg v. Ohio – Overturned the 1919 Schenck v. United States decision and stated instead that speech was protected by the First Amendment unless it represented "imminent lawless action."

1971 – Lemon v. Kurtzman – The 1971 case of Lemon vs. Kurtzman was important in establishing the limits to which government institutions and religious institutions could influence one another. The case involved a Rhode Island law which allowed state schools to subsidize the salaries of teachers in private, religious schools. The court ruled unanimously that this was in violation of the Establishment Clause of the Constitution – a clause which prohibits any government acts to establish a "state religion." The case resulted in a three-pronged test now used by courts in determining whether a law is in violation of the First Amendment right to freedom of religion. The first of the three prongs, or standards, of the test is that a statute must have a secular, legislative purpose. This is also known as the purpose prong, and ensures that religious agendas are not the motivating factor behind a law. The second prong, also known as the effect prong, is that the statute may not advance or prohibit religious practice. Lastly, the third prong, or en**tanglemen**t prong, states that a statute may not result in an excessive government entanglement with religious affairs.

1973 – Roe v. Wade – Determined that the government can not restrict a woman's ability to get an abortion after the first trimester.

Due Process

The topic of the judicial branch of government at both the state and federal level also requires a discussion of the right to due process which is guaranteed to every citizen through the Constitution.

Americans are most familiar with the due process rights granted to them by Amendment VI which include the following:

- The right to have counsel
- The right to have the case heard by a jury of one's peers
- The right to a speedy and public trial
- The right to know what the crime and the evidence is
- The right to have witnesses appear
- The right to question the witnesses

The Constitution also provides other rights relating to due process. Article I prevents the use of a bill of attainder which would allow a person to be convicted without a trial and makes it unconstitutional to pass ex post facto laws which would allow people to be arrested for something they did in the past which is now illegal. Article I also ensures the right of habeas corpus, which means the individual who is accused must appear in court and must know the charges against him or her.

Amendment V also provides due process protection by preventing double jeopardy so a person who is found innocent cannot be tried again for the same crime. The amendment also protects individuals from having to testify against themselves. When defendants say "I'll take the fifth" they are referring to the protection against self-incrimination provided by this amendment.

One of the most important rights is that "individuals are innocent until proven guilty" which means that they retain all of their civil rights until they are found guilty of a crime. In some countries, the reverse is true and individuals who are arrested are considered guilty until they are proven to be innocent. Regardless of the idea that people cannot be viewed as guilty until the completion of a trial, the media has made it difficult for that feeling to be maintained by the public. In high profile cases this is particularly true, such as with the O. J. Simpson case, when many people had made up their mind regarding his guilt before the trial had even started thanks to constant publicity in newspapers and on television.

Stare Decisis

Despite the fact that the judicial branch of the government does not have power to make or pass laws, this branch still wields a significant amount of power. To a large extent it is the judicial branch that interprets how laws are to be enforced. With a complex system of court hierarchies that flow through both state and federal channels it is important that uniformity is maintained throughout the nation. For this reason the principle of stare decisis is important. Stare decisis means that a court is obligated to adhere to precedent, particularly rulings made by higher courts. If a similar case has already been heard then the court will issue the same ruling. Occasionally, decisions will be overturned when appealed to higher courts in which case a new precedent is set.

Law-Making Process

The three branches of government work together to create, interpret, and enforce laws. However, the creation of those laws requires a very specific process that can be lengthy.

Not every bill that comes to Congress eventually becomes a law. In fact, nearly 20,000 bills are proposed but only about 1/5 of those ever become laws.

A bill can be introduced by either a member of the House of Representatives or the Senate with some exceptions. For example, if the bill is going to involve taxation, then it must be introduced in the House of Representatives because the Constitution gives them power over that issue. Although the bill must be introduced by a member of Congress, it can be written by anyone, including private citizens.

After the bill is introduced, it is assigned to one of 22 committees in the House of Representative by the Speaker of the House. Each committee is concerned with specific issues, such as commerce or education. The committee discusses the bill and decides what actions to take next. If they decide to table the bill, the bill will not be voted on by the House of Representatives. If it is "reported out," the bill will then be placed on a calendar along with other bills that are awaiting some type of action.

The next step is for the bill to be read in its entirety by the House of Representatives so that they can vote on it. If the bill receives a simple majority of the votes, then it can move on to the Senate for consideration.

In the Senate, the process is very similar. A Senator must introduce the bill, and then it will be assigned to one of 14 different committees. The committee will decide how to proceed with the bill. If they decide to table the bill, then it will not be voted on even though it has passed in the House of Representatives.

Bills that are "reported out" by the Senate committees are heard by the Senate in the order they arrive generally and according to their schedule. Specific types of legislation are only discussed on certain days. This can lead to a phenomenon known as filibustering. In the Senate, there can be unlimited debate over a proposed bill, so a member of the minority party can speak against the bill so long that the Senate will not have time to vote on it on that day.

When and if the Senators are able to vote on the bill, a simple majority is all that is needed to approve it.

Even though a bill only needs a simple majority of votes in both Houses to reach this stage, there are a number of factors that influence its chances of succeeding. One of those factors is known as logrolling. In logrolling, Senator A may vote in favor of or against a bill as a favor to another Senator B. The Senator B will then repay the favor through his or her votes on a bill or issue that is of special interest to Senator A.

Another factor that influences voting is lobbyists. Lobbyists work for different organizations, such as unions or the NRA (National Rifle Association). They are paid individuals whose job is to convince Congress members to vote one way or another on bills. They can sway the Legislators votes because the organizations they represent may later fund their campaigns or provide other favors. While lobbyists can make it possible for groups without much political power to have their voices heard by the government, many people believe that lobbyists and the organizations they represent simply have too much input into the process of law-making today.

The last two factors are the President and the constituents. If the President has a strong interest in a bill, he may appeal to Congress to vote in the manner he wishes. Constituents can also contact their Congressional leaders directly to let them know their feelings about the vote. Legislators know that if they vote against a bill the majority of their constituents favor or vice versa, then they may have a tougher time getting re-elected so they tend to listen when the voters speak in their districts.

In some cases, the bill that was voted on by the House of Representatives and by the Senate may not be identical. If this occurs, the bill will go into a committee made up of members from both Houses who will discuss the differences and work towards creating a single bill that both groups can agree upon. After this is completed, the bill is sent to the President.

When the President receives the bill, he has several options on how to proceed. First, he can do nothing. If he does not sign or veto the bill within ten days, the bill automatically becomes law. He also has the option of signing the bill in order to make it a law.

Finally, the President can veto the bill. When this occurs, the bill has to go back to the House of Representatives for another vote. This time around the bill requires two-thirds of the votes to be in its favor for it to proceed to the Senate for a similar vote. If the bill receives two-thirds of the votes in both Houses, then it becomes a law. If it does not, then the bill is considered dead and no more action can be taken on it.

Election Process

One of the most important rights a citizen has in the United States is the right to vote. When the Constitution was first written, voting was an important part of the government that the Founding Fathers wanted to establish. However, some groups were not included in the definition of "voters" in the 18th century, including African-Americans and women. Since that time, the Constitution has been amended to allow all men and women over the age of 18 to vote.

Despite changes to the Constitution, some states attempted to pass laws that would indirectly prohibit some groups of people, particularly African Americans, from being able to vote. One of those methods was the poll tax which was a tax an individual paid when they went to vote. Since many African Americans could not afford to pay the tax, they were not allowed to vote. Poll taxes were made unconstitutional in 1964 with the passage of Amendment XXIV.

Other methods were also used to prevent African Americans and other groups from voting. Literacy tests were given at polling places which required potential voters to read a passage from the Constitution; the white poll workers selected the passage to be read, thus many African Americans were given more difficult passages to read than those white voters were given. The Grandfather Clause was also used for a similar purpose. According to the Clause, you were able to vote if your grandfather had voted in an election. Because most African Americans' ancestors were slaves who had not been allowed to vote, they were not given their right to vote because of the Clause.

Voting was clearly important to both groups. Those who wanted to prevent African Americans (and later other groups, such as Asian immigrants) from voting were afraid that their influence in the election would have a negative impact on the status quo. African Americans and other minority groups, including women, realized that voting was the main way they could bring about political change and ensure their rights were protected.

Despite the importance of voting in the United States, turnout is generally low. Today, nearly half of all registered voters do not vote during presidential elections. Even less vote during non-presidential elections for local leadership or Congressional representation. There are a number of reasons proposed for this "voter apathy," but most people who do not vote do not believe their vote matters and/or are dissatisfied with the choices available to them in the election.

Fundraising

In the United States, fundraising plays a huge role in getting a candidate elected to public office. Candidates raise money in a variety of ways. Billboards, lawn signs, mail, email, leaflets, and phone banks are all ways to get the word out. Candidates can host fund-raisers, throw parties, and look for donations from interest groups (like unions, businesses, religious groups, ethnic groups) who support the candidate's views. When fundraising and campaigning, the candidate demonstrates how people will benefit personally from the candidate being elected. Because money is such an important factor in elections, there are limits on how much an individual or a group can donate to a candidate.

Political Parties

Nothing in the Constitution requires the formation of political parties, but the idea of creating them is just as old. The first two political parties were the Federalists who supported the adoption of the Constitution and the Anti-Federalists who worried that the Constitution gave too much power to the centralized government.

Since then, parties have been formed by individuals who share common political ideologies. Parties make it easier to organize political power. For example, the party that has a majority in Congress has more control over which bills are passed.

Political parties also make it simpler for individuals to make voting choices. Most individuals identify with one party and that identification guides their voting decisions.

For the most part, those choices are between the two parties of the United States: the Democrats and the Republicans. Candidates from both of these parties are assured inclusion on all ballots during elections. They also receive the vast majority of the votes.

The Democratic Party began back in 1794 with Thomas Jefferson. However, the party was known as the Republican Party at the time. Most people today refer to it as the

Democratic-Republican Party to prevent confusion, but during Jefferson's time it was simply known as the Republican Party. Until Andrew Jackson's presidency, between 1829-1837, the party was the only real force in politics. During Jackson's leadership, the party split into two. Jackson's faction of the party eventually became known as the Democratic Party.

Today's Republican Party is actually not as old. Its first convention was held in 1854. Many of their original members had actually belonged to the Whig party that was by then defunct because of internal disagreements over slavery laws. In the beginning, the Republican Party worked hard to protect the interests of workers, farmers, and slaves. Abraham Lincoln, for example, was a Republican president. As society changed, so did the Republican Party.

Typically, Democrats are concerned with social welfare and providing money for education, health care, and other services that directly impact the needs of citizens. Republicans are concerned with keeping capitalism strong and thriving in the country through deregulation and tax breaks. Both parties have very different stands on issues such as abortion, gun control, and gay rights. However, the most recent election showed that those differences are fading as the Democratic Party attempts to stay in the center of the political spectrum.

Besides the two major parties in the United States, other smaller parties often appear on the ballots as well. These parties include the following:

Libertarian Party – This party, which was founded in 1971, believes in a hands-off approach by government. They want unregulated capitalism; social freedom with government imposed restrictions (including the legalization of drugs); free trade with foreign countries; and limited military usage. The most basic principle of libertarianism is a commitment to liberty. The views of the Libertarian party center on ensuring for the freedoms of life, liberty, and property. They reject any use of force or violence against individuals, and uphold socially liberal policies. Freedom of choice and autonomy are very important in libertarian philosophy. In terms of their economic views, libertarians advocate an open market with laissez-faire operations. They advocate low taxation, and in some cases the dissolution of the Internal Revenue Service entirely. Libertarians are very fiscally conservative and believe that government involvement should be kept to a minimum.

Green party – While the party was first organized in 1984, many other countries, including Germany, already had very strong Green parties. In general, these parties are dedicated to preserving the environment, providing for the needs of citizens, using non-violent solutions instead of military ones, and promotion of a grassroots democracy.

Constitution Party – Originally called the U.S. Taxpayer's Party when it was formed in 1992, this party's main focus is on preserving the Constitution and adhering to it in a strict way. Members typically believe in a strong connection between religion and politics and are more right wing when it comes to social issues, such as immigration laws.

Not all names on the ballot have to come from a party, however. In 1992, Ross Perot made a name for himself and brought a mild resurgence to the idea of a third option for president (outside of the main two parties). He was even allowed to participate in the presidential debates and ended up winning 19% of the popular vote, which was an unheard of amount for an independent candidate. Three years after the election, he formed the Reform party and ran as a candidate in the 1996 elections but did not perform as well. Although not supported by Perot, former wrestler Jesse Ventura ran for governor of Minnesota as the Reform Party candidate and won in 1998. The Reform Party is no longer an active political party in most parts of the country, and Ross Perot is no longer affiliated with the party.

Presidential Candidate Selection

Because the United States is primarily a two-party system, the candidate selection method used by those parties is the one most people recognize. Within each party, a number of candidates make it known that they are interested in pursing a spot on the ballot in November. These candidates then begin competing with one another through appearances and advertisements.

During primary elections, voters from each party get to choose from among the potential candidates for their party. A Democrat, for example, would only select from the Democratic candidates. Primary elections are held at different times in different states usually beginning in March and lasting through June. Some states do not have primary elections at all because they are too expensive and there is not enough voter turnout.

After the primary season is over and each party determines which candidate has received the most votes, the candidate must be officially nominated. Each party holds a separate convention during the summer. These conventions are multi-day events with celebrities and other political leaders, but the main objective is to publicly announce who will run for president during that election year. Generally, the nomination does not surprise any one but the convention makes it official and allows for the beginning of the campaign.

Third parties usually have conventions as well to nominate their candidates, but they are not automatically placed on ballots like the candidates from the main two parties. If they received enough votes during the previous election, they are automatically listed on the ballot. That rarely occurs, however. Instead, most third-parties have to work hard in each state to get their parties listed on the ballots and each state has different requirements, such as the number of signatures needed.

Presidential Elections

While most political leaders in the United States are selected by popular vote, the President is chosen through the Electoral College which the Founding Fathers created and added to the Constitution in Article II. They were concerned that the citizens of the fledgling United States would not be able to make an informed choice regarding who should wield executive power, but they wanted the people to have a say as to whom that person would be. The Electoral College was a compromise between those two ideas.

When voters go to the polling place every four years on the first Tuesday of November and choose a candidate for president, they are actually voting for a group of individuals known as Electors. These people have been selected by their parties to serve an important function in the election process.

The number of Electors varies from state to state. Each state receives one electoral vote for each Senator and Representative it has in Congress. Amendment XXIII also gave the District of Columbia electors. Currently, they have three electors because of their population. The combination of all these electors means that there are 538 electoral votes up for grabs during the election.

In 48 states (excluding Maine and Nebraska), the candidate who receives the most popular votes in the election receives all of that state's electoral votes. In Maine and Nebraska, they can divide up their electors based on popular vote, although they have not had to do this in an election so far.

Forty-one days after the general election, the electors in each state go to their state's capital to vote once for president and once for vice-president. While they are expected to vote for the candidate they represent, they are under no obligation to do so in many states. Some states take the issue very seriously and have made it a misdemeanor crime for an elector to vote for a different candidate.

On that day, the votes are collected, sealed in an envelope, and sent to the current Vice-President in his role as head of the Senate. When Congress meets in January, the envelopes are unsealed and the results are counted. The candidate for president and the vice-president who receive a majority of electoral votes (270 votes currently) is declared the winner.

If no candidate receives a majority, then the matter is turned over to Congress. The House of Representatives decides who becomes president while the Senate votes for the vice-president. Senate voting is done normally, and the candidate who receives a simple majority is considered the winner. In the House of Representatives, the individuals vote by state. Each state gets one vote, and the legislators from each state must decide whom to vote for. If they are evenly divided between the candidates, then they abstain from voting. The candidate who receives a simple majority in the House of Representatives becomes president. Voting in both Houses continues until a candidate is selected by the majority.

Because the voting progress could possibly extend beyond the official Presidential Inauguration date of January 20th, the Constitution states the either the newly elected vice-president (if that vote has been decided) or the Speaker of the House will be acting President until Congress makes a selection.

Congressional Elections

Elections for Senators and Representatives are not as complicated. Every two years, the members of the House of Representatives and 1/3 of the Senators are elected by popular vote in November. On their own, these elections don't generate much public interest and turnout is usually quite low.

Voting Decisions

All political parties have a definite interest in figuring out what makes voters choose the candidates they do. By understanding what motivates constituents, the parties can try to run candidates and engage in campaigning that will give them an edge in the election.

One of the biggest influences on voters is environment. Typically, people endorse one party over another. When they vote, they vote along party lines. As a result, children are influenced by their parent's political affiliation and usually grow up to vote for the same political party.

Another aspect of environment is location. For example, a person living in New York City, which is strongly Democratic, might be influenced to vote for Democratic candidates because that's one of the ways they identify themselves with their city.

Another reason for the voting choices individuals make in November is known as a litmus test. Each person has some key issues that they feel strongly about. For example, someone might be pro-life and feel that issue is a top priority for the country to deal with. That person would make their voting decisions primarily on whether or not a candidate shared his or her pro-life stance. In recent years, issues such as abortion, gun control, gay rights, and prayer in school have all been used to help voters make their decisions.

A candidate's personality and appearance also play a role in voter decisions. People want to vote for someone who seems down-to-earth, likable, and trustworthy. When Al Gore was running for president in 2000, for example, many people criticized him for his lifeless presentations, and his lack of a winning personality may have hurt him in the election. On the other, Ronald Reagan who was president between 1980 and 1988 was considered to appear extremely honest and friendly in-person and on television. His personality helped him to become one of the most popular presidents in the United States during the 20th century.

Appearance is also said to have been an influence on voters, particularly since the introduction of televised debates. In 1960, John F. Kennedy and Richard Nixon engaged in what was known as "the Great Debate." Seventy million people were able to watch the debate for the first time on television. The interesting thing about the debate was that people who had heard the debate on the radio proclaimed Nixon the winner while individuals who had watched the debate on television believed Kennedy had clearly won. Many of those viewers simply believed that Kennedy appeared more confident, more trustworthy, and more presidential. Thus, he won the election. Since then there have been concerns that televised debates encourage viewers to focus on candidates' appearances instead of on their stance on key issues.

Interestingly enough, none of these issues seem to matter as much to who gets elected as the answer to the question "Who already holds the office?" Incumbents have a significant advantage in both the Presidential and the Congressional elections. In fact, 90% of incumbents in the House of Representatives and Senate are re-elected. Major changes in voter attitude or a significant scandal related to that political leader are the only things that give an opponent a fighting chance to win the seat.

The advantage incumbents have is not difficult to understand. They have a longer time to make a positive impression on constituents than their challengers. Plus, they are given the franking privilege, which means they can use the mail for free to send out materials to voters in their area. They typically have more funds to use for campaigns, as well.

Most Americans seem to favor term limits for Congressional leaders similar to those which are placed on the presidential office. Currently, a member of Congress can run an unlimited number of times. That means making changes in Congressional leadership can be difficult.

During the 1980's and 1990's, the issue of term limits was a much-debated topic. Many states began passing laws limiting the number of terms for their own Congressional leaders. In 1995, the Supreme Court voted that the states did not have the power to set or enforce term limits on federally elected leaders. Term limits could only be set through the passage of an amendment to the Constitution. Congress did attempt to pass such an amendment in 1995, but it did not receive enough votes. In subsequent years, members of Congress have been publicly opposed to setting terms limits.

Soft Money

Soft money is money that is donated to a political party for the purpose of party building activities, rather than being donated directly to a candidate. The benefit of such donations is that they are far less regulated than are direct, or hard money, contributions. Soft money contributions can be made by individuals, corporations, committees, and essentially any other entity that so desires. The donations are also not limited by federal regulations. The only stipulation is that the funds cannot be used to promote a specific candidate. Because of this, they are often used to advocate the beliefs of the party or to show the opposing candidate in negative light.

Hard Money

Hard money is money that is donated to a specific candidate for the purpose of supporting their election. These donations have historically been tightly regulated. For example, hard money donations can be made only by individuals or Political Action Committees (PACs). Corporations, businesses, non-profit organizations, and others are legally banned from making such donations. Furthermore, the amounts which can be donated are limited. As a result, soft money is an essential supplement to most campaigns.

Interest Groups

Modern politics are strongly influenced by the power of interest groups. These groups are created when people who share similar characteristics decide to join forces in order to create a more powerful force. While many groups do work towards educating the public about the issues they feel are most important, the groups are primarily interested in having their voices heard by legislators.

There is a wide array of interest groups in modern American society. Some are professional organizations, such as the Teamsters or the American Medical Association. Others are civil rights organizations such as the NAACP and the National Organization of Women. There are also religion-oriented interest groups like the National Council of Churches and single-issue interest groups like the National Rifle Association (NRA).

Interest groups who want to influence legislators hire lobbyists, who are well-made individuals with a background in law and experience in Washington. The lobbyist's job is to communicate the wishes of the interest group to members of Congress. For example, if a bill related to malpractice law was being voted on, then lobbyists from the American Medical Association would be working hard to sway Congressional leaders so that they will vote in a way that is favorable to the doctors the lobbyist represents.

The reason lobbyists are so successful is because leaders need the approval and backing of these large interest groups in order to win elections. Interest group support equals money.

Political Action Committees (PACs) are organizations that donate money to political campaigns. Since the amount of money which can be donated by an individual is limited, PACs allow individuals to get more money for their donation. For example, one person may donate $1000 to a politician but such a small amount (most campaigns cost millions of dollars, especially the presidential ones) delivers no real benefit for the donator. However, when that same $1000 is given to a PAC and is combined with the $1000 donated by another 25,000 members, then the politicians are going to listen. Most PACs are associated with large interest groups.

Lobbyists and PACs have been criticized because many people believe they are taking control of the government away from the constituents. Others explain that PACs and lobbyists ensure that the average person can have his or her concerns heard by the politicians in Washington.

Some steps have been taken to at least keep track of lobbyist activity. In 1946, the Federal Regulation Lobbying Act was passed and it required all lobbyists to register with the Clerk of the House of Representatives and the Secretary of the Senate. In 1978, the Ethics in Government Act was passed to prevent former political officials from becoming lobbyists within the first two years of leaving office. Additionally, there has been talk about limiting the amount of money PACs can raise and contribute.

Another interest group issue is that not all of these groups are based in the United States and not all of them represent individuals. Countries and corporations can also serve as interest groups and can hire lobbyists to influence Congressional voting. Of course, neither of these entities may be working for the best interest of the citizens of the United States. These types of lobbyists and interest groups have also created a great deal of debate, but no laws have been passed to prevent them from continuing their efforts.

Elite Theory

Elite theory is the belief that nearly all political power is held by a relatively small and wealthy group of people with similar core values, interests, and goals. A single elite, as opposed to a variety of competing groups, decides important issues for the nation as a whole, leaving relatively minor matters for the middle level and almost nothing for the common person. Because the elite holds the power, policies tend to disproportionately favor the elite over everyone else. Their power is based on their personal economic resources and high positions in big corporations. They do not depend upon the ability to gain public support by representing or protecting the interests of other larger social groups. The elite theory system creates an imbalance of power that America's government tries to avoid.

Public Opinion & the Media

In a democracy, the desires of the majority are supposed to guide the actions of the government. However, those people working in the government need an accurate method of understanding those desires. That's why understanding and shaping public opinion has been so important to politicians.

Public opinion is influenced by many factors, such as environment, socioeconomics, education, race, gender, and religion. All of these factors combine to shape the way we perceive events. However, the media has become increasingly influential in shaping public opinion as well.

Since the beginning of politics in the United States, the media has played a useful role in keeping citizens informed on the issues. In the early days, pamphlets and articles were published, such as the Federalist letters and anti-slavery literature. Because communication was limited in those days, these types of printed resources were critical to having educated voters.

Over time, the media's role has grown. Today, people can learn about politics on the Internet, on the television, in newspapers, in books, on the radio, and in periodicals. They have ready access to more information than ever, but many people are troubled by the quality and reliability of that information in recent years.

The First Amendment provides for a free press because the Founding Fathers believed this was critical for a successful democracy. During the Watergate scandal in the early 1970's, citizens found out how true that was.

Watergate refers to a number of scandals that occurred during Richard Nixon's presidency and which he was aware of. One of those scandals involved wire-tapping the offices of the Democratic National Committee in the Watergate hotel. Two reporters – Bob Woodward and Carl Bernstein for the Washington Post, along with help from an informant, broke the story which eventually led to Nixon's resignation. Without the work of the press, the criminal activity may never have been brought to light.

Unfortunately, many people believe that the drive to find the truth and even the ability to report is has been lessened by the modern media. Five corporations own the majority of television and print media. For example, Time Warner owns the WB network, Turner Broadcasting, CNN, and more than a dozen other channels as well as publishing companies and web sites. Meanwhile GE owns NBC, CNBC, and another dozen channels. Plus, some channels are jointly owned by two or more of these giant corporate entities.

Opponents to this type of control point out that these corporations are going to want the news to be reported in a manner that is favorable to them. For instance, since GE is also one of the world's largest arms manufacturers and a leading maker of medical equipment, the company may not want reporters at NBC to promote an end to wars or ways to decrease rising health care costs. They may also suppress news stories which may portray them in a negative light.

Others see nothing wrong with the centralized control of the media and believe that the competition between the five companies will continue to keep the news reliable and comprehensive.

Regardless of how one views the media, it does shape the perceptions and opinions of the public. People are always strongly influenced by those they see as leaders. Through the media, the President can influence the voters to support his policies, for example.

Campaign advertising is another example of media influence. The widespread use of television commercials, which are often extremely negative, has had a dramatic impact on modern elections. During the 1988 presidential elections, George Bush's campaign showed television commercials about a convicted criminal named Willie Horton who killed a woman while he was on furlough. Michael Dukakis, Bush's opponent, was the governor of Massachusetts during that incident and Bush was able to use the ads to make Dukakis seem "soft on crime" which was a major issue during that election. Bush easily defeated Dukakis in the election thanks in great part to the way those ads influenced the public's view of his opponent.

Ad campaigns and other types of media influence are not necessarily bad, but some people do worry that if news channels become less objective and more biased toward one political party or issue, then they can misuse their power and can manipulate public opinion. These types of claims have already been used against the Fox News Corporation. However, the best way to deal with those possibilities is through an educated public that is taught how to critically analyze all arguments to determine which ones are the most effective and rational.

Democracy and Economics

Democracy implies no specific doctrine of economics. Democratic governments have embraced committed socialists and free marketers alike. Indeed, a good deal of the debate in any modern democracy concerns the proper role of government in the economy. Nevertheless, it would be fair to say that the proponents of democracy generally regard economic freedom as a key element in any democratic society. This fact has not precluded economic issues from becoming the chief force dividing, and defining, the "left-right" political spectrum as we know it today.

Social democrats, for example, have stressed the need for equality and social welfare as the core of the government's economic policies. In the past, this has entailed government ownership of the major components of the nation's economy, such as telecommunications, transportation, and some heavy industry. They also call upon government to provide medical, unemployment, and other welfare benefits to those in need. By contrast, centrist and conservative political parties usually place much greater stress on the free-market economy, unimpeded by government control or intervention, as the most effective means of achieving economic growth, technological progress, and widespread prosperity.

Virtually all sides in the economic debate, however, share a greater common ground than they might concede in the heat of political argument. For example, both left and right accept the important role played by a free labor movement, independent of government. Workers in a free society have the opportunity to form or join unions to represent their interests in bargaining with employers on such issues as wages, health and retirement benefits, working conditions, and grievance procedures.

No contemporary democratic state has an economic system that is either completely state-owned or totally free of government regulation. All are mixtures of private enterprise and government oversight. All rely heavily on the workings of a free market, where prices are set not by the government but by the independent decisions of thousands of consumers and producers interacting each day.

Political parties on the left, while generally social democratic in orientation, recognize that the free market, acting in accordance with the principles of supply and demand, is the primary engine of economic growth and prosperity. Similarly, center-right parties, while generally opposed to government intervention or ownership of production, have accepted the government's responsibility for regulating certain aspects of the economy: providing unemployment, medical, and other benefits of the modern welfare state; and using tax policy to encourage economic development. As a result, modern democracies tend to have economies that, while diverse in the details, share fundamental features.

In recent years, the collapse of centrally planned economies in many parts of the world has reinforced the emphasis on the critical role of free markets. In economic as in political affairs, it seems, the indispensable element remains freedom. As Morris Abram, former U.S. ambassador to the United Nations Human Rights Commission and now chairman of UN Watch in Geneva, has said, "Freedom alone may not guarantee economic success. But repression most certainly guarantees economic failure." Even in those rare cases where authoritarian regimes have made significant economic strides, they have done so by granting the freedom in the economic realm that they deny their citizens politically. Moreover, their success generally has not strengthened the hand of the regime over the long term but has contributed, as in the case of Chile and Taiwan, to demands by the people for political freedom commensurate with their economic freedom.

Democracies will continue to debate economic issues as vigorously in the future as in the past. But increasingly, the debate is focusing not on the failed alternative of state-run command economies but on ensuring the benefits of the free market for all in an increasingly interdependent world.

The government can also use the power of **eminent domain**. This gives countries the right to seize a person's personal property for government use and/or for the government to give it to a third party to be used for "public use." Some but not all states require that the person be compensated for their property. Eminent domain is usually used for public utilities, streets, sidewalks, railroads, etc.

Laissez-faire

The term laissez-faire is a French term that roughly translates as "let it alone." It is used to describe economic systems in which there are no government restrictions, and open trade is allowed. The concept of laissez-faire economy derives from the work of economic philosopher Adam Smith. In his book The Wealth of Nations, Smith lays forth a belief that economies are naturally self-regulating. This is because individuals are naturally driven to seek profits. Therefore, according to Smith, if an economy is left unregulated the participants in that economy will naturally reach the most efficient possible outcomes in terms of production, pricing, and other economic factors. Although there is typically some level of government involvement in the economy, the United States is considered one example of a laissez-faire economy. This was particularly true during the industrial revolution when capitalism was strong and the economy was growing rapidly. Alternatively, in periods of economic downturn it is common for the federal government to pass regulations that seek to solve problems through regulation.

The Iron Triangle

Iron triangles are the closed, mutually supportive relationships that are formed between government agencies, special interest groups and activists, and legislative committees with jurisdiction over that area (Congress, interest groups, and bureaucratic agencies). These groups use their combined influence to gain control over a particular area of government policy. As long as they have the same goals, the members of these small groups tend to dominate all policy-making in an area. They can also present a unified front against "outsiders" who attempt to establish policies the "insiders" disagree with.

Revolving Door Politics

Historically the corporate and legislative fields have been highly connected. It is not unusual for high- or mid-level government officials to transition into corporate positions following their release from government positions, and vice versa. This practice is known as revolving door politics. Although the phenomenon is beneficial in that it allows for qualified and experienced individuals to be placed in important government and corporate roles, it is also a cause for concern in many cases. This is because such close connections between government and corporate individuals increases possibilities for favoritism, and corrupt practices.

Sample Test Questions

1) Which amendment protects against search and seizure?

   A) 1st Amendment
   B) 2nd Amendment
   C) 3rd Amendment
   D) 4th Amendment
   E) 5th Amendment

The correct answer is D:) 4th Amendment.

2) Which of the following cases supported freedom of the press?

   A) New York Times Co. v. Sullivan
   B) Lochner v. New York
   C) Mapp v. Ohio
   D) Korematsu v. United States
   E) Dred Scott v. Sanford

The correct answer is A:) New York Times Co. v. Sullivan. The Supreme Court ruled that actual malice must be proved for a printed criticism of a public official to be considered libel.

3) The Department of Commerce does which of the following?

   A) Manage supply and demand
   B) Creates standards of measure
   C) Manages pricing
   D) Improves technology for small businesses
   E) None of the above

The correct answer is B:) Creates standards of measure.

4) In which case did the Supreme Court rule that evidence obtained illegally cannot be used in court?

A) Mapp v. Ohio
B) McCulloch v. Maryland
C) Korematsu v. United States
D) Miranda v. Arizona
E) Lochner v. New York

The correct answer is A:) Mapp v. Ohio. Mapp's home had been searched without the officers first obtaining a warrant, and she was convicted (of a different crime than they originally wished to prove) based on the evidence they collected.

5) Which group of people most recently received the right to vote?

A) Women
B) African Americans
C) Asian Americans
D) Americans between the age of 18 and 21
E) Latin Americans

The correct answer is D:) Americans between the age of 18 and 21.

6) Which of the following terms describes the process and legal proceedings of a lawsuit?

A) Gerrymandering
B) Casework
C) Reapportionment
D) Mugwump
E) Litigation

The correct answer is E:) Litigation.

7) Which Supreme Court case supported the idea of "separate but equal" in relation to segregation?

   A) Bowers v. Hardwick
   B) Plessy v. Ferguson
   C) Roe v. Wade
   D) Lemon v. Kurtzman
   E) Miranda v. Arizona

The correct answer is B:) Plessy v. Ferguson.

8) Which clause forbids Congress from passing a law requiring all citizens to be a member of a specific church?

   A) Comity Clause
   B) General Welfare Clause
   C) Guarantee Clause
   D) Establishment Clause
   E) Elastic Clause

The correct answer is D:) Establishment Clause. The Establishment Clause prohibits Congress from passing laws "respecting an establishment of religion."

9) What was the only amendment of the constitution to be repealed?

   A) 5th Amendment
   B) 10th Amendment
   C) 13th Amendment
   D) 18th Amendment
   E) 1st Amendment

The correct answer is D:) 18th Amendment.

10) Which clause allows Congress to collect taxes to pass any laws that they deem necessary?

   A) Elastic Clause
   B) Uniformity Clause
   C) Reserved Powers Clause
   D) Uniformity Clause
   E) General Welfare Clause

The correct answer is A:) Elastic Clause. The Elastic Clause allows Congress to pass all laws considered necessary and proper to perform their responsibilities.

11) Which of the following is NOT a civil liberty protected by the constitution?

A) Freedom of speech
B) Right to bear arms
C) Due process
D) Freedom of religion
E) None of the above

The correct answer is E:) None of the above.

12) Which governmental branch has the right to interpret the constitution, laws, and treaties?

A) Legislative
B) Executive
C) Judicial
D) A and B combined
E) Any of the branches

The correct answer is C:) Judicial. This power is often called judicial review.

13) Which of the following does NOT lobby Congress?

A) Unions
B) Foreign governments
C) Teacher's coalitions
D) Private businesses
E) Political parties

The correct answer is E:) Political parties.

14) Which case resulted in the practice of reading of Miranda rights?

A) Marbury v. Madison
B) Gideon v. Wainright
C) Miranda v. Arizona
D) Garcia v. San Antonia
E) McCulloch v. Maryland

The correct answer is C:) Miranda v. Arizona. Miranda got set free because he hadn't been informed of his constitutional right to consult an attorney.

15) The most influential aspect in determining what a person's political party/affiliation will be is

A) Peers
B) Family
C) Church
D) Neighborhood
E) School

The correct answer is B:) Family.

16) The Gramm-Rudman-Hollings Act gave Congress the right to dismiss the Comptroller General, a financial officer appointed by the president. This was ruled unconstitutional because the position requires executive powers to enforce laws. Therefore, it was ruled unconstitutional in the case of

A) Bowers v. Hardwick
B) Ferguson v. Skrupa
C) Gideon v. Wainright
D) Bowsher v. Synar
E) McCulloch v. Maryland

The correct answer is D:) Bowsher v. Synar.

17) The court case of Brown v. Board of Education resulted in

A) Allowing abortion
B) Desegregating schools
C) Small business reform
D) Creating standard student per instructor ratio
E) None of the above

The correct answer is B:) Desegregating schools.

18) The Supreme Court determined that the federal courts have the right to determine the constitutionality of voting districts in which case?

A) Mapp v. Ohio
B) Baker v. Carr
C) Lochner v. New York
D) McCulloch v. Maryland
E) Miranda v. Arizona

The correct answer is B:) Baker v. Carr. Baker felt that the voting districts allotted unfair advantage to rural areas because they had lower populations. The districts were supposed to be reconsidered each time there was a census, but they hadn't been. The state argued that the matter shouldn't be considered in court because it was a legislative problem.

19) What is cloture?

A) The time the President has to sign or veto a bill.
B) A time limit placed on how long a bill can be considered by the Senate.
C) A time limit placed on how long a bill can be considered by the House of Representatives.
D) The time it takes for a bill to be voted on.
E) The time within a bill must be passed between houses in Congress.

The correct answer is B:) A time limit placed on how long a bill can be considered by the Senate. Cloture was designed to avoid attempts to block or delay Senate action on a bill by debating it at length.

20) __________ is NOT an example of congressional oversight.

A) Senate trials
B) House of representatives impeachment trials
C) Preventing fraud
D) Overturn Supreme Court decisions
E) None of the above

The correct answer is D:) Overturn Supreme Court decisions.

21) If the Congressman from Minnesota agrees to vote for the Congressman from Arizona's bill about seat belts laws only if he votes for his bill on new minimum wages it would be called

A) Realignment
B) Litigation
C) Gerrymandering
D) Logrolling
E) Casework

The correct answer is D:) Logrolling. Logrolling is when two congress members agree to vote for one another's unrelated bills.

22) AARP is the __________ interest group in the United States.

A) Largest
B) 2nd largest
C) 3rd largest
D) 4th largest
E) 5th largest

The correct answer is A:) Largest.

23) In which case did the Supreme Court rule that Kansas had the right to determine the legality of "debt adjusting" because its legality was a legislative issue and not a judicial one?

A) Gideon v. Wainright
B) Ferguson v. Skrupa
C) Plessy v. Ferguson
D) Bowsher v. Synar
E) Baker v. Carr

The correct answer is B:) Ferguson v. Skrupa. The Supreme Court overturned a lower court in their decision to allow the practice.

24) Which department is in charge items such as the National Parks Service?

A) Department of Defense
B) Department of State
C) Department of the Interior
D) Environmental Protection Agency
E) Department of Justice

The correct answer is C:) Department of the Interior.

25) Which of the following was NOT done during the Constitutional Convention of 1787?

A) Abolish the Articles of Confederation.
B) Creation of a system of two chamber legislation.
C) Creation of a three branch governmental system.
D) Creation of a system of representation based solely on population.
E) Determination of three fifths representation of slaves in taxation and population count.

The correct answer is D:) Creation of a system of representation based solely on population. Answers A, B, C, and E are all true of the decisions made in the Constitutional Convention in 1787.

26) Double jeopardy means

A) You are never liable to pay double taxes
B) You cannot be tried for the same crime twice
C) You have the right to bear arms
D) You cannot cheat on your taxes twice without criminal penalty
E) None of the above

The correct answer is B:) You cannot be tried for the same crime twice.

27) Which of the following terms describes voters who do not identify themselves with any one party?

A) Incumbents
B) Litigates
C) Carpetbaggers
D) Mugwumps
E) None of the above

The correct answer is D:) Mugwumps.

28) Anyone above age ___ can register to and vote.

A) 16
B) 18
C) 19
D) 21
E) 25

The correct answer is B:) 18.

29) After the Revolutionary War, what was the governing document of the United States?

A) Declaration of Independence
B) Constitution of the United States
C) Magna Carta
D) Articles of Confederation
E) None of the above

The correct answer is D:) Articles of Confederation. The Articles created a weak national government which proved ineffective. It wasn't until 11 years after the Declaration of Independence that the Constitution was finally written.

30) Which Supreme Court case determined that a tomato was classified as a vegetable, not a fruit?

A) Bowers v. Hardwick
B) Plessy v. Ferguson
C) Roe v. Wade
D) Nix v. Hedden
E) Miranda v. Arizona

The correct answer is D:) Nix v. Hedden.

31) Which group was the first to be granted the right to vote?

A) Black males
B) Black females
C) Felons
D) 18 year olds
E) Native Americans

The correct answer is A:) Black males. Males of all races were granted the right to vote under the 15th Amendment in 1870.

32) From which document is the following phrase an excerpt from?

"The powers not delegated to the United States by the Constitution, nor prohibited by it to the states, are reserved to the states respectively, or to the people."

A) Constitution
B) Bill of Rights
C) Declaration of Independence
D) Federalist Papers
E) None of the above

The correct answer is B:) Bill of Rights. The quote is the 10th Amendment.

33) The number of a state's electoral votes is calculated by

A) Number of registered voters
B) Population
C) Amount of representatives in the House of Representatives
D) Amount of square miles in the state
E) None of the above

The correct answer is B:) Population.

34) Which of the following terms describes a change in public opinion?

A) Logrolling
B) Reapportionment
C) Litigation
D) Gerrymandering
E) Realignment

The correct answer is E:) Realignment. This is because the opinions are shifted or re-aligned.

35) Anyone who wants to run for President must be at least ____ years old.

A) 18
B) 21
C) 25
D) 35
E) 45

The correct answer is D:) 35.

36) A Writ of Habeas Corpus protects against which of the following?

A) Individuals being held for long periods of time without trial.
B) Individuals being held without charge.
C) Individuals being given cruel or unusual punishments for crimes.
D) Individuals being discriminated against by the Federal Government.
E) A Writ of Habeas Corpus does not protect against any of the above.

The correct answer is B:) Individuals being held without charge. Because of Habeas Corpus, individuals must be informed of what they are being charged with.

37) What is the difference between Republicans and Democrats?

A) Republicans believe in minimal government, Democrats believe in a large role of government
B) Republicans are conservative, Democrats are liberal
C) Republicans are more concerned with the good of the individual, Democrats are more concerned with the good of society as a whole
D) None of the above
E) All of the above

The correct answer is E:) All of the above.

38) What is the main task of the Solicitor General?

A) To enforce the Civil Rights Acts
B) To coordinate and facilitate communication between federal agencies
C) To review the programs and personnel of the federal agencies
D) To supervise and conduct government litigation in the United States Supreme Court
E) All of the above

The correct answer is D:) To supervise and conduct government litigation in the United States Supreme Court. The Solicitor General represents the federal government in cases before the Supreme Court.

39) Jim Crow laws enforced

A) Public schooling
B) Segregation
C) The right to vote
D) Reproductive rights
E) Drug sentence maximums

The correct answer is B:) Segregation.

40) A grant which is awarded to a state for the general use in education is a

A) Provisional Grant
B) Block Grant
C) Categorical Grant
D) Specific Grant
E) General Grant

The correct answer is B:) Block Grant. A block grant is money awarded to a state by the Federal Government with general provisions on how it is to be used.

41) Who generally has more power in the Senate?

A) The VP
B) Majority leader
C) Minority leader
D) President pro tempore
E) None of the above

The correct answer is D:) President pro tempore.

42) The court case of Miranda v. Arizona resulted in

A) Allowing abortion
B) Desegregating schools
C) Small business reform
D) Creating standard student per instructor ratio
E) Citizens being reminded of their rights when arrested

The correct answer is E:) Citizens being reminded of their rights when arrested.

43) When and where was the Constitutional Convention held?

A) Independence Hall, 1776
B) Liberty Hall, 1787
C) Carpenters Hall, 1776
D) Liberty Hall, 1776
E) Independence Hall, 1787

The correct answer is E:) Independence Hall, 1787. The Declaration of Independence was signed in the same place 11 years prior (1776).

44) Which of the following is NOT true of fundraising in political elections?

A) Fundraising plays a huge role in getting a candidate elected to public office.
B) There is no limit to how much a candidate can raise for a single campaign.
C) Candidates raise money in a variety of ways.
D) There are limits on how much an individual or a group can donate to a candidate.
E) All of the above

The correct answer is E:) All of the above.

45) The Iron Triangle typically refers to

A) The President, interest groups, and bureaucratic agencies
B) Bureaucratic agencies, Congress, and the President
C) Law enforcement agencies, the President, and Congress
D) Interest groups, bureaucratic agencies, and law enforcement agencies
E) Congress, interest groups, and bureaucratic agencies

The correct answer is E:) Congress, interest groups, and bureaucratic agencies. Groups in the "iron triangle" used their combined influence to gain control over a particular area of government policy.

46) Which amendment protects against quartering soldier troops?

A) 1st Amendment
B) 2nd Amendment
C) 3rd Amendment
D) 4th Amendment
E) 5th Amendment

The correct answer is C:) 3rd Amendment.

47) Which governmental branch has the right to declare war?

A) Legislative
B) Executive
C) Judicial
D) A and B combined
E) Any of the branches

The correct answer is A:) Legislative. The legislative branch is the sole law making body. They also declare war, impeach the president, and review presidential appointments.

48) What is Writ of Certiorari?

A) A case the Supreme Court reviews
B) The decision the Supreme Court makes on a case
C) A petition the Supreme Court makes for a lower court to hand up a case for review
D) A petition a lower court makes for the Supreme Court to review a case
E) The grant of a petition for the Supreme Court to review the decision of a lower court

The correct answer is E:) The grant of a petition for the Supreme Court to review the decision of a lower court. When a person is not satisfied with the ruling on a case, they may petition the Supreme Court to review the decision. If they grant this petition, it is called a Writ of Certiorari.

49) An incumbent representative is

A) Someone's family member running for office
B) Someone running for an office they currently hold
C) Hiring someone related to you
D) The Governor appoints them
E) None of the above

The correct answer is B:) Someone running for an office they currently hold.

50) Social contract theory is the view that a person's political and moral obligations depend on a "contract" formed by the society in which they live. According to John Locke, what is the basis for creating this social contract?

A) Establishing laws
B) Protection of property
C) Diminishing violence committed in a state of nature
D) A desire to belong to a group
E) All of the above

The correct answer is B:) Protection of property. In Locke's argument for civil government, private property is created when a person mixes his labor with raw materials in nature. Because nature belongs to no one, a system is created to define and protect property.

51) Which case established that state enforced segregation was legal?

A) Baker v. Carr
B) Plessy v. Ferguson
C) MuCulloch v. Maryland
D) Garcia v. San Antonio
E) Brown v. Board of Education

The correct answer is B:) Plessy v. Ferguson. This decision was later overturned by Brown v. Board of Education.

52) Who is the head of the House of Representatives?

A) The Speaker of the House
B) The Vice President
C) The President pro tempore
D) The majority leader
E) The minority leader

The correct answer is A:) The Speaker of the House.

53) The President must be a natural born citizen of the United States and reside in the U.S. for how many years?

A) 2
B) 10
C) 14
D) 20
E) 25

The correct answer is C:) 14.

54) Which of the following cases promoted the power of the Federal Government over state governments by declining the right of state's to tax the national bank?

A) Roe v. Wade
B) Lochner v. New York
C) Mapp v. Ohio
D) MuCulloch v. Maryland
E) Plessy v. Ferguson

The correct answer is D:) MuCulloch v. Maryland. At the time, James MuCulloch was the head of the bank and refused to pay the Maryland tax.

55) Which of the following argued for balanced government powers?

A) John Locke
B) Sir Isaac Newton
C) Benjamin Franklin
D) David Hume
E) Baron de Montesquieu

The correct answer is E:) Baron de Montesquieu.

56) An incumbent is

A) A person who promotes the illegal practice of redrawing voting districts to give one party or person an unfair advantage.
B) A person who brings a case to trial.
C) A person who tracks and monitors shifts and changes in public opinion.
D) A person who currently holds an office.
E) None of the above

The correct answer is D:) A person who currently holds an office. For example, a current congress member is an incumbent.

57) The Bill of Rights includes

A) The first 5 amendments
B) The first 10 amendments
C) The first 15 amendments
D) The first 20 amendments
E) All the amendments

The correct answer is B:) The first 10 amendments.

58) Federalism is the process by which each citizen is under

A) The authority of a central national government.
B) The authority of a regional state government.
C) The authority of a local city government.
D) The authority of both a national and state government.
E) The authority of both a national and city government.

The correct answer is D:) The authority of both a national and state government. The United States operates under a federal system where people are citizens of both the nation (under the Federal Government) and a state (under the individual state governments).

59) Stare decisis is closely related to what principle?

A) Constitutionality
B) Good faith
C) Proof
D) Precedence
E) None of the above

The correct answer is D:) Precedence. "Stare decisis" is Latin for "to stand by things decided." The Court generally stands by decisions it has previously made.

60) Federal district court judges are nominated by

A) The citizens they serve
B) The President
C) The Chief Justice
D) Any senator
E) None of the above

The correct answer is B:) The President.

61) Which of the following is NOT related to citizen's voting rights?

A) The 19th Amendment
B) The 22nd Amendment
C) The 23rd Amendment
D) The 24th Amendment
E) The 26th Amendment

The correct answer is B:) The 22nd Amendment. The 22nd Amendment prevents the president from being elected twice. The rest apply to black voting rights, women's voting rights, poll taxes, and voting rights in the District of Columbia.

62) If the Federal Government grants a state money, but it must be used for the math program in high schools, and must go towards buying technology, is most likely a

A) Provisional Grant
B) Block Grant
C) Categorical Grant
D) Specific Grant
E) General Grant

The correct answer is C:) Categorical Grant. A categorical grant is money awarded to a state by the Federal Government with specific provisions and extensive restrictions on how it is to be spent.

63) What is the difference between civil liberties and civil rights?

A) Civil liberties are a protection against negative government action, civil rights are positive actions the government takes on citizen's behalf.
B) Civil rights are a protection against negative government action, civil liberties are positive actions the government takes on citizen's behalf.
C) Not everybody has civil liberties because they apply only in some circumstances, civil rights are general rights.
D) You always have civil rights, but your civil liberties can be suspended.
E) There is no difference, civil rights and civil liberties are the same.

The correct answer is A:) Civil liberties are a protection against negative government action, civil rights are positive actions the government takes on citizen's behalf.

64) What is the goal of affirmative action?

A) Protecting civil liberties
B) Reducing discrimination
C) Reducing poverty
D) Reducing the unemployment rate
E) Reducing government influence on daily life

The correct answer is B:) Reducing discrimination. Affirmative action describes programs which seek to reduce or reverse the effects of discrimination, as opposed to merely "not practicing" it.

65) The promise of a future vote in exchange for an unrelated vote is called

A) Mud slinging
B) Pork grinding
C) Log-rolling
D) Barn-raising
E) None of the above

The correct answer is C:) Log-rolling.

66) The Comity Clause

A) Prohibits Congress from passing laws "respecting an establishment of religion."
B) Allows Congress to pass all laws considered necessary and proper to perform their responsibilities.
C) Declares that all taxes must be uniform throughout the United States.
D) Allows Congress to collect taxes to be used for the protection and general welfare of the citizens.
E) Explains that citizens of one state have the same rights as citizens of other states.

The correct answer is E:) Explains that citizens of one state have the same rights as citizens of other states.

67) Which position is responsible for the supervising federal elections at the state level?

A) The Governor
B) The Secretary of State
C) The State Treasurer
D) The Lt. Governor
E) None of the above

The correct answer is B:) The Secretary of State.

68) What was decided in Roe v. Wade?

A) The government can not restrict a woman's ability to get an abortion at any stage of pregnancy.
B) An abortion can be legally performed during the first trimester.
C) An abortion may only be performed in special circumstances (if the mother's life is at stake, in cases of rape, etc.).
D) An abortion may only be performed in special circumstances (if the mother's life is at stake, in cases of rape, etc.) and only during the first trimester.
E) Abortions are illegal regardless of circumstance or stage of pregnancy.

The correct answer is B:) An abortion can be legally performed during the first trimester.

69) How the New Deal affected Federalism in America

A) The New Deal created a system of cooperative federalism
B) The New Deal gave the states more independence than ever before
C) The New Deal gave the government more influence than ever before
D) The New Deal created the "new federalism" concept
E) The New Deal did not affect federalism in America

The correct answer is C:) The New Deal gave the government more influence than ever before. The New Deal gave rise to a number of federal-run programs like Social Security. Until this time, this was exclusively run by the states.

70) If the government wanted to build a freeway across an area where there were houses, which of the following statements is TRUE?

A) They could force the people to move and build the freeway there without compensating them.
B) They would be able to take the land whether or not the people wanted to sell, as long as they gave fair compensation.
C) They would not legally be able to force the people to move, and would have to choose a different spot to build the freeway.
D) Unless they offered the people at least twice market value, they would not legally be allowed to force them to sell their homes.
E) They would have no power to force the people to sell their houses.

The correct answer is B:) They would be able to take the land whether or not the people wanted to sell, as long as they gave fair compensation. This is called eminent domain.

71) Which amendment guarantees the right to free speech?

A) 1st Amendment
B) 2nd Amendment
C) 3rd Amendment
D) 4th Amendment
E) 5th Amendment

The correct answer is A:) 1st Amendment.

72) Why did Montesquieu argue for a separation of powers?

A) To prevent corruption
B) To provide checks and balances
C) To make the government run more efficiently
D) A and B
E) B and C

The correct answer is D:) A and B. Montesquieu argued that the best way to secure liberty and prevent a government from becoming corrupted was to divide the powers of government among different actors who would check each other.

73) Which case established that states must provide an attorney in criminal cases where one cannot be afforded?

A) MuCulloch v. Maryland
B) Ferguson v. Skrupa
C) Bowsher v. Synar
D) Lochner v. New York
E) Gideon v. Wainright

The correct answer is E:) Gideon v. Wainright.

74) What is an executive agreement?

A) A formal alliance between the United States and a foreign government.
B) A treaty between the United States and a foreign government.
C) A legally binding agreement between the United States and a foreign government that does not have the approval of the Senate.
D) A relatively informal but still politically binding agreement between the United States and a foreign government.
E) An informal agreement between the United States and a foreign government that is neither legally nor politically binding.

The correct answer is D:) A relatively informal but still politically binding agreement between the United States and a foreign government It is less formal than a treaty and is not subject to the constitutional requirement for ratification by two-thirds of the U.S. Senate.

75) Presidential approval ratings generally

A) Get better throughout the term
B) Get worse throughout the term
C) Stay the same throughout the term
D) Increase halfway through the term
E) None of the above

The correct answer is B:) Get worse throughout the term.

76) What is the main difference between the House and Senate in the Federalist papers?

A) The total number of representatives
B) How representatives are elected and their term length
C) They are essentially in charge of different parts of the lawmaking process
D) All of the above
E) None of the above

The correct answer is D:) All of the above. Senators are given longer terms so they are less concerned with being reelected and more concerned with the greater good and making laws to benefit in the future. House Representatives have shorter terms and are more concerned with pleasing the public's immediate demands.

77) In the Mcculloch v. Maryland case, it was decided that Congress ______ have the power to create The Second Bank of the United States and Maryland ______ have the power to tax the bank.

A) Did; did
B) Did; did not
C) Did not; did
D) Did not; did not
E) None of the above

The correct answer is B:) Did; did not. Congress claimed the right to incorporate a bank under the Necessary and Proper clause in the Constitution.

78) In the case of Gibbons v. Ogden the Supreme Court ruled that who had the authority to regulate interstate commerce?

A) President
B) States
C) Congress
D) Judges
E) Individuals

The correct answer is C:) Congress. In the case, Congress had licensed an interstate company which operated in waters that the state of New York had granted exclusive rights to.

79) Which of the following were the authors of The Federalist Papers?

A) Alexander Hamilton & John Jay
B) James Madison
C) Thomas Jefferson
D) Both A & B
E) Both B & C

The correct answer is D:) Both A & B.

80) Elite theory is the political theory that

A) All political power is held in the top branches of the government.
B) The elite class sways and often controls the political opinion of the lower classes.
C) Nearly all political power is held by a relatively small and wealthy group of people with similar core values, interests, and goals.
D) Political power is held by a select few who are the top of their class and are equally representative of all ethnic, spiritual and economical denominations.
E) Powerful political positions tend to be held by members of the elite class because their core values, interests, and goals strongly influence those of the lower class.

The correct answer is C:) Nearly all political power is held by a relatively small and wealthy group of people with similar core values, interests, and goals.

81) Which of the following people was NOT an author of the Federalist Papers?

A) Alexander Hamilton
B) James Madison
C) John Jay
D) Thomas Jefferson
E) All of the above were involved in writing the Federalist Papers

The correct answer is D:) Thomas Jefferson. Thomas Jefferson wasn't even in the country when the Constitution was written or passed. He was the ambassador to France at the time.

82) Which amendment protects against being held without charges, and protection from double jeopardy?

A) 1st Amendment
B) 2nd Amendment
C) 3rd Amendment
D) 4th Amendment
E) 5th Amendment

The correct answer is E:) 5th Amendment.

83) If a bill is sent to the president and is not signed within ten days what happens?

A) It is considered to be vetoed
B) It dies and must be reintroduced
C) It is returned to Congress to be revised
D) It becomes a law as if it had been signed
E) None of the above

The correct answer is D:) It becomes a law as if it had been signed. According to the pocket veto clause, the president may veto a bill if he does not wish to sign it. If the bill is not vetoed or signed within ten days (not including Sundays) it becomes a law.

84) The number of representatives in the House of Representatives is a constant 435. Because the number each state receives is based on population, what must occur after each federal census?

A) Gerrymandering
B) Casework
C) Reapportionment
D) Realignment
E) Litigation

The correct answer is C:) Reapportionment. Reapportionment is redistribution of congressional seats after each census.

85) The census occurs every ___ years.

A) 2
B) 5
C) 10
D) 15
E) 18

The correct answer is C:) 10.

86) Which of the following is NOT an element of the Lemon test?

A) The legislation must have a non religious purpose.
B) The legislation must promote a variety of religions.
C) The legislation must not result in excessive government involvement in religion.
D) The legislation must not have the main goal of harming or helping religion.
E) Both B and D

The correct answer is B:) The legislation must promote a variety of religions. It shouldn't promote religion. The legislation must not harm or favor any one religion.

87) Which Supreme Court case ruled that the government cannot for a person to hold specific religious beliefs?

A) Torcaso v. Watkins
B) Baker v. Carr
C) Roe v. Wade
D) Lemon v. Kurtzman
E) Miranda v. Arizona

The correct answer is A:) Torcaso v. Watkins.

88) The Constitution consists of which type of powers?

A) Implied
B) Divided
C) Express
D) Regular
E) Natural

The correct answer is C:) Express. The Constitution specifically explains the rights and powers of each branch.

89) Bicameral

A) Consists of three legislative branches
B) Consists of two legislative branches
C) Is another word for absentee ballot
D) Is a term limit
E) None of the above

The correct answer is B:) Consists of two legislative branches.

90) In which case did the Supreme Court rule that a woman has the right to choose an abortion under the implied right to personal privacy?

A) Lochner v. New York
B) Roe v. Wade
C) Mapp v. Ohio
D) Ferguson v. Skrupa
E) Baker v. Carr

The correct answer is B:) Roe v. Wade.

91) Which Supreme Court case raised debate on the right of privacy?

A) Bowers v. Hardwick
B) Baker v. Carr
C) Roe v. Wade
D) Lemon v. Kurtzman
E) Miranda v. Arizona

The correct answer is A:) Bowers v. Hardwick.

92) Which case affirmed the legality of internment camps during World War II?

A) Roe v. Wade
B) Lochner v. New York
C) Mapp v. Ohio
D) MuCulloch v. Maryland
E) Korematsu v. United States

The correct answer is E:) Korematsu v. United States. The Supreme Court ruled that the need for protection outweighed Korematsu's individual rights.

93) Which amendment guarantees the right to bear arms?

A) 1st Amendment
B) 2nd Amendment
C) 3rd Amendment
D) 4th Amendment
E) 5th Amendment

The correct answer is B:) 2nd Amendment.

94) Which of the following is NOT a right mentioned in the Bill of Rights?

A) Freedom, Speech, Press, and Assembly
B) Protection against illegal search and seizure
C) Citizens cannot be forced to house troops during peace times
D) Protection against cruel and unusual punishment
E) All of the above are mentioned in the Bill of Rights

The correct answer is E:) All of the above are mentioned in the Bill of Rights. Answer A is the first amendment, answer B is the fourth amendment, answer C is the third amendment, and answer D is the eighth amendment.

95) The Writ of Habeas Corpus helps uphold which amendment of the constitution?

A) 4
B) 5
C) 12
D) 15
E) 18

The correct answer is B:) 5.

96) Which of the following terms describes the practice of organizing voting districts to favor one political group?

A) Gerrymandering
B) Casework
C) Reapportionment
D) Realignment
E) Litigation

The correct answer is A:) Gerrymandering. The practice of gerrymandering originated in 1812 with Massachusetts Governor Elbridge Gerry and is illegal.

97) Which of the following was the first ever created Executive department?

A) Labor
B) Commerce
C) Defense
D) State
E) Transportation

The correct answer is D:) State.

98) Which case established the power of judicial review?

A) Baker v. Carr
B) Plessy v. Ferguson
C) Gideon v. Wainright
D) Marbury v. Madison
E) Miranda v. Arizona

The correct answer is D:) Marbury v. Madison. The court ruled that Marbury's claim was invalid because it was based on an unconstitutional law.

99) Which governmental branch has the right to enforce laws?

A) Legislative
B) Executive
C) Judicial
D) A and B combined
E) Any of the branches

The correct answer is B:) Executive. The power of the Executive Branch lies with the President. His responsibility is to implement and enforce laws.

100) Who is the head of the Senate?

A) The Speaker of the House
B) The Vice President
C) The President pro tempore
D) The majority leader
E) The minority leader

The correct answer is B:) The Vice President.

101) What is popular sovereignty?

A) The belief that what is best for the group is more important than what is best for the individual.
B) The belief that people who live in a region voluntarily create government systems to meet their needs.
C) The belief that governments only exist with the consent of the governed.
D) The belief that the ultimate power to make laws belongs to the people.
E) The belief that there is no "divine right," that the people get to choose who their rulers are.

The correct answer is D:) The belief that the ultimate power to make laws belongs to the people.

102) Which Supreme Court case supported the free speech of students and teachers in public school?

A) Bowers v. Hardwick
B) Tinker v. Des Moines
C) Roe v. Wade
D) Lemon v. Kurtzman
E) Miranda v. Arizona

The correct answer is B:) Tinker v. Des Moines.

103) Which case established that segregation in public schools was unconstitutional?

A) Brown v. Board of Education
B) Roe v. Wade
C) Plessy v. Ferguson
D) MuCulloch v. Maryland
E) Baker v. Carr

The correct answer is A:) Brown v. Board of Education. This overturned the case of Plessy v. Ferguson which allowed "separate but equal" schools.

104) Which of the following is America's form of government?

A) Monarchy
B) Aristocratic
C) Socialist
D) Republican
E) Parliamentary

The correct answer is D:) Republican.

105) Which of the following cases affirmed the power of eminent domain?

A) Hawaii Housing Authority v. Midkiff
B) Bowsher v. Synar
C) Garcia v. San Antonio Transit Authority
D) Baker v. Carr
E) Korematsu v. United States

The correct answer is A:) Hawaii Housing Authority v. Midkiff. The case confirmed the state of Hawaii's right to redistribute privately held lands. The majority of the state's lands were in the hands of a few citizens, creating an oligopoly harmful to the economy.

106) Popular sovereignty was promoted by

A) John Locke
B) Sir Isaac Newton
C) Benjamin Franklin
D) David Hume
E) Baron de Montesquieu

The correct answer is A:) John Locke.

107) Which of the following correctly identifies the succession to the presidency following the death or removal of the president?

A) Vice President, Secretary of State, Speaker of the House, President Pro Tempore of the Senate.
B) Vice President, President Pro Tempore of the Senate, Secretary of State, Speaker of the House.
C) Vice President, Speaker of the House, President Pro Tempore of the Senate, Secretary of State.
D) Vice President, Speaker of the House, Secretary of State, President Pro Tempore of the Senate.
E) Vice President, Secretary of State, President Pro Tempore of the Senate, Speaker of the House.

The correct answer is C:) Vice president, Speaker of the House, President Pro Tempore of the Senate, Secretary of State.

108) The First Amendment does not cover

A) Sexual content
B) Obscenity
C) Flag burning
D) Protests
E) None of the above

The correct answer is B:) Obscenity.

109) Which clause in the Constitution allows Congress to regulate trade between states?

A) Comity Clause
B) Elastic Clause
C) Commerce Clause
D) Reserved Powers Clause
E) General Welfare Clause

The correct answer is C:) Commerce Clause. The Commerce Clause allows Congress to regulate trade with foreign nations and between individual states.

110) The act of negative campaigning against a political opponent is called

A) Mud slinging
B) Pork grinding
C) Log-rolling
D) Barn-raising
E) None of the above

The correct answer is A:) Mud slinging.

111) Which case supported slavery by declaring that slaves had no right to sue because they were property?

A) Roe v. Wade
B) Baker v. Carr
C) Dred Scott v. Sanford
D) Ferguson v. Skrupa
E) Lochner v. New York

The correct answer is C:) Dred Scott v. Sanford. Scott had attempted to sue for his freedom after his owner moved to a free state from a slave state.

112) Which Supreme Court case ruled that the government cannot restrict abortion?

A) Torcaso v. Watkins
B) Baker v. Carr
C) Roe v. Wade
D) Lemon v. Kurtzman
E) Miranda v. Arizona

The correct answer is C:) Roe v. Wade.

113) In the case of Locher v. New York the Supreme Court ruled that

A) The Supreme Court affirmed that Congress has the right to impose minimum wage and overtime pay.
B) The Supreme Court ruled that states have the right to enforce segregation in schools on the basis of "separate but equal" doctrine.
C) States could not limit the number of hours worked a week because they couldn't interfere with a person's right to enter into an employment contract.
D) The Supreme Court ruled that a woman has the right to choose an abortion under the implied right to personal privacy.
E) The Supreme Court determined that the federal courts do have the right to determine the constitutionality of voting districts.

The correct answer is C:) States could not limit the number of hours worked a week because they couldn't interfere with a person's right to enter into an employment contract.

114) Which trait is unrelated to influencing political party preference?

A) Gender
B) Race
C) Intelligence
D) Economic status
E) Education

The correct answer is C:) Intelligence.

115) The following is a quote from which document?

"We hold these truths to be self-evident, that all men are created equal, that they are endowed by their Creator with certain unalienable rights, that among these are life, liberty and the pursuit of happiness."

A) Declaration of Independence
B) Constitution
C) Gettysburg Address
D) Bill of Rights
E) Federalist Papers

The correct answer is A:) Declaration of Independence. The Declaration of Independence was passed by the Second Continental Congress in 1776.

116) This Department was once united with the Department of Commerce

A) Justice
B) Labor
C) Defense
D) Health
E) Energy

The correct answer is B:) Labor.

117) Which of the following describes the outcome of Garcia v. San Antonio Transit Authority?

A) The Supreme Court determined that the federal courts do have the right to determine the constitutionality of voting districts.
B) The Supreme Court ruled that states could not limit hours worked in a week because they couldn't interfere with a person's right to enter into an employment contract.
C) The Supreme Court affirmed that Congress has the right to impose minimum wage and overtime pay.
D) The Supreme Court ruled that states are required to provide an attorney in criminal cases where the defendant cannot afford one.
E) None of the above

The correct answer is C:) The Supreme Court affirmed that Congress has the right to impose minimum wage and overtime pay. This overturned a previous ruling that minimum wage and overtime pay could only be dictated in government related areas.

118) What is a presidential mandate?

A) An order that comes directly from the President
B) An order for the President that comes from Congress
C) The President's responsibility to fulfill his promises to the people
D) The President's main objective or responsibility
E) None of the above

The correct answer is C:) The President's responsibility to fulfill his promises to the people. When a President receives a significant majority of votes he is said to have received a "mandate" to pursue the promises he made to the people in the campaign that resulted in the significant victory.

119) A state senator who served on an energy committee while in office is later hired by energy companies to lobby for their interests. This is an example of

A) Corporate connectedness
B) Sovereign immunity
C) Monopolism
D) Libertarianism
E) Revolving door politics

The correct answer is E:) Revolving door politics. It is not unusual for high- or mid-level government officials to transition into corporate positions following their release from government positions, and vice versa.

120) The amendment allowing people to vote at 18 instead of 21 happened in what year?

A) 1961
B) 1964
C) 1967
D) 1971
E) None of the above

The correct answer is D:) 1971.

121) Which of the following terms is defined as a congressional representative's efforts to help a constituent resolve a problem with the federal bureaucracy?

A) Gerrymandering
B) Casework
C) Reapportionment
D) Realignment
E) Litigation

The correct answer is B:) Casework.

122) Which of the following groups are allowed to make hard money contributions to political campaigns?

A) Non-profit organizations
B) Businesses
C) Corporations
D) Individuals
E) All of the above

The correct answer is D:) Individuals. Hard money is money that is donated to a specific candidate for the purpose of supporting their election. These donations have historically been tightly regulated. Businesses, non-profit organizations, and others are legally banned from making such donations.

123) Because of the War Powers Resolution, the President

A) Is required to have permission from Congress to deploy armed forces regardless of circumstances.
B) Has limited ability to deploy armed forces.
C) Can deploy troops without consent from Congress if the United States is threatened.
D) Has the full and exclusive authority to deploy armed forces.
E) None of the above

The correct answer is B:) Has limited ability to deploy armed forces. The War Powers Resolution was passed to limit the power of the president to deploy military forces without the consent of Congress, but it also gives guidelines for if this happens.

124) In the case of Regents of the University of California v. Bakke, the Supreme Court ruled what about race requirements in university admissions?

A) That any form of affirmative action program was constitutional.
B) That specified quota requirements based on race are unconstitutional.
C) That the Supreme Court did not have the constitutional right to make a decision in the case.
D) That specified quota requirements were the only constitutional affirmative action program.
E) None of the above

The correct answer is B:) That specified quota requirements based on race are unconstitutional. However, they did claim that correctly designed affirmative action programs could be constitutional, just not specified requirements.

125) The symbol of the Republican party is an

A) Elephant
B) Donkey
C) Snake
D) Giraffe
E) None of the above

The correct answer is A:) Elephant.

126) According to the Supremacy Clause in the Constitution

A) State law must be followed even if it conflicts with federal law.
B) Both state and federal law must be followed under all circumstances.
C) Although federal law much be followed, state laws are optional.
D) Federal law must be followed even if it conflicts with state law.
E) None of the above

The correct answer is D:) Federal law must be followed even if it conflicts with state law. This is because the Federal Government and Constitution is deemed the "supreme law of the land."

127) When the President removes criminal charges is called

A) Probation
B) Parole
C) Pardon
D) Reduced
E) None of the above

The correct answer is C:) Pardon.

128) Who is the least likely to vote?

A) High income brackets
B) Low income brackets
C) Minorities
D) Young adults
E) The elderly (over 65)

The correct answer is D:) Young adults.

129) What is not a traditional use of land seized under eminent domain powers?

A) Public utilities
B) Streets and sidewalks
C) Schools
D) Railroads
E) None of the above

The correct answer is E:) None of the above. All are examples of uses of land seized under eminent domain. Eminent domain is the power to seize personal property for government or public use.

130) During what era did the dual federalism system decline in the United States?

A) Reconstruction
B) Civil Rights
C) WWI
D) Great Depression
E) WWII

The correct answer is D:) Great Depression. In an attempt to ease the economic turmoil of the Great Depression, many federal programs were enacted that brought the federal government into supremacy in the lives of most people.

131) Equal rights between state governments and federal governments is an indication of which system?

A) Presidential mandate
B) Dual federalism
C) Anarchy
D) Socialism
E) None of the above

The correct answer is B:) Dual federalism. Dual federalism refers to governments in which power is equally divided between two groups. This is exactly the type of system that was created by the separation of duties between the federal government and the various state governments.

132) Which of the following preemptively forbids an individual from publishing certain things?

A) Prior restraint
B) The first amendment
C) Establishment Clause
D) Supremacy Clause
E) Solicitor general

The correct answer is A:) Prior restraint. Prior restraint is a practice of forbidding the publishing of certain materials before they have been published. The US Supreme Court has ruled the practice of prior restraint to be one of the most serious violations of the first amendment (which protects the freedom of speech).

133) Which of the following BEST describes the theory of laissez-faire economies?

A) Strict government regulations are necessary for healthy economies
B) Individuals are selfless so the economy will function well with or without regulation
C) Economies are naturally self-optimizing and government regulations destroy that
D) Without regulations a capitalist economy will lead to monopolies and inflation
E) None of the above

The correct answer is C:) Economies are naturally self-optimizing and government regulations destroy that. Supporters of laissez-faire economies argue that individuals are naturally driven to seek profits. Therefore, if an economy is left unregulated the participants in that economy will naturally reach the most efficient possible outcomes in terms of production, pricing, and other economic factors.

134) A case is brought to a judge that is almost identical to one that was previously heard. The judge will likely make the same ruling due to the principle of

A) Res ipsa loquitur
B) In personam
C) Stare decisis
D) Establishment
E) Supremacy

The correct answer is C:) Stare decisis. Stare decisis means that a court is obligated to adhere to precedent. If a similar case has already been heard then the court will issue the same ruling.

135) Who is responsible for representing the interests of the United States government in court?

A) Secretary of State
B) President of the Senate
C) Speaker of the House
D) Solicitor General
E) Supreme Court

The correct answer is D:) Solicitor General. The Solicitor General is the attorney who represents the interests of the United States in court. He is directly below the Attorney General in ranking.

136) Which of the following is mandated by the War Powers Act?

A) No military conflict can continue longer than 60 days unless Congress approves it
B) Congress must ask for the permission of the President to make a declaration of war
C) Only the President can hold the title of Commander in Chief
D) The Judicial Branch holds the power to issue a declaration of war
E) None of the above

The correct answer is A:) No military conflict can continue longer than 60 days unless Congress approves it. The purpose of the Act is to require collaboration between Congress and the President any time warfare is imminent. It requires that no military conflict can continue longer than 60 days unless Congress approves it and issues a declaration of war.

137) The War Powers Act was passed in response to which war?

A) Civil War
B) Vietnam War
C) WWI
D) War of 1812
E) Korean War

The correct answer is B:) Vietnam War. When President Nixon engaged in the long and taxing Vietnam War without the approval of Congress, Congress quickly passed the War Powers Act in an attempt to prevent future administrations from doing the same thing.

138) Which of the following is NOT true of soft money?

A) Corporations can make soft money contributions
B) The amount of contributions an individual can make are limited
C) Funds classified as soft money contributions can only be used for party building activities
D) Soft money donations can be used to advocate party platforms
E) All of the above are true

The correct answer is B:) The amount of soft money contributions an individual can make are limited. Hard money contributions are tightly limited which is why the unregulated, soft-money contributions are so important to candidates.

139) Which of the following would indicate the existence of a Presidential Mandate?

A) A public announcement from the White House
B) A clause in the Constitution which indicates one
C) A candidate receiving a significant majority of votes
D) An ongoing lawsuit involving the executive branch
E) None of the above

The correct answer is C:) A candidate receiving a significant majority of votes. Essentially the Presidential Mandate is the responsibility that the new President has to fulfill the promises he made to voters. A President is said to have a mandate from the people when he has received a significant majority of the votes in an election.

140) Which constitutional clause establishes the Constitution as the supreme law of the land?

A) Establishment Clause
B) Supremacy Clause
C) Enumerated powers Clause
D) Embellishment Clause
E) Federalist Clause

The correct answer is B:) Supremacy Clause. This clause states that the Constitution is the "supreme law of the land." In practice, the Supremacy Clause has been interpreted to mean that the powers of the federal government are higher than the powers of state governments.

141) Precinct is the ______ geographic area in a voting area.

A) Smallest
B) Largest
C) Most diverse
D) Most represented
E) None of the above

The correct answer is A:) Smallest.

142) Which of the following best describes Libertarianism?

A) Socially liberal and fiscally conservative
B) Socially liberal and fiscally liberal
C) Socially conservative and fiscally liberal
D) Socially conservative and fiscally conservative
E) None of the above

The correct answer is A:) Socially liberal and fiscally conservative. Libertarians favor socially liberal policies while rejecting government spending and taxation.

143) What are the two general types of grants awarded by the federal government to local governments?

A) Category based grants and general grants
B) Block grants and circular grants
C) Open grants and closed grants
D) Block grants and categorical grants
E) None of the above

The correct answer is D:) Block grants and categorical grants. The reason that two types of grants have developed is because of the federal structure of the government. Block grants allow for more open distribution of grants whereas categorical grants allow the government more control.

144) The House Ways and Means committee is in charge of what?

A) Taxes
B) Social security
C) Unemployment benefits
D) Medicare
E) All of the above

The correct answer is E:) All of the above.

145) If a grant has a narrow scope and tightly regulated use, it is a

A) Regulatory grant
B) Block grant
C) Categorical grant
D) Local grant
E) Enumerated grant

The correct answer is C:) Categorical grant. Categorical grants are money distributions which a state can elect to accept, but they are not required to. The terms for using these types of grants are dictated by the federal government, and generally they are very specific.

146) Which of the following is NOT a standard of the lemon test?

A) A statute must have a secular legislative purpose
B) A statute must not advance or prohibit religious practice
C) A statute must allow and encourage the practice of religion
D) A statute must not result in an excessive government entanglement with religious affairs
E) All of the above are standards of the Lemon Test

The correct answer is C:) A statute must allow and encourage the practice of religion. The lemon test is a three-pronged test for determining whether a law is in violation of freedom of religion. Answers A, B, and D comprise the three standards of the test.

147) Which test is used in determining whether a law is in violation of freedom of religion?

A) Sliding bar test
B) Evasion test
C) Motivation test
D) Supremacy test
E) Lemon test

The correct answer is E:) Lemon test. The lemon test was developed through the case of Lemon vs. Kurtzman. In the case, the court ruled that the state of Rhode Island could not subsidize religious schools, and developed the lemon test as a guideline for future laws that could possibly violate freedom of religion.

148) Which group of individuals was first granted the legal right to vote?

A) Native Americans
B) African Americans
C) Women
D) Both A and B
E) Both B and C

The correct answer is B:) African Americans. Although voting restrictions in many southern states prevented African Americans from voting, the legal right for former slaves to vote was granted in 1870. Women were given the right to vote in 1920, and Native Americans were granted that right in 1924.

149) The fact that cases against the United States government are heard in federal courts shows that which of the following principles is not abided by?

A) Due process
B) Sovereign immunity
C) Supremacy
D) Civil rights
E) Stare decisis

The correct answer is B:) Sovereign immunity. The doctrine of sovereign immunity is that political leaders are immune from lawsuits. The fact that the United States government is routinely involved in court cases shows that this is not the case in the United States.

150) Which of the following was the most influential in allowing for the expansion of civil rights laws?

A) Supremacy Clause
B) Integration Clause
C) Equal Protection Clause
D) Establishment Clause
E) Due Process Clause

The correct answer is C:) Equal Protection Clause. The Equal Protection Clause is a clause in the Fourteenth Amendment which states that all people must be given equal protection of the law. The Supreme Court took a narrow interpretation of this clause to overturn many unfavorable Reconstruction-era laws that allowed for further discrimination.

151) How many electors comprise the Electoral College?

A) 50
B) 100
C) 385
D) 435
E) 538

The correct answer is E:) 538. The Electoral College is the institution that elects the president based on the popular vote in each respective state. A candidate must receive 270 electoral votes to win the election.

Test-Taking Strategies

Here are some test-taking strategies that are specific to this test and to other CLEP tests in general:

- Keep your eyes on the time. Pay attention to how much time you have left.
- Read the entire question and read all the answers. Many questions are not as hard to answer as they may seem. Sometimes, a difficult sounding question really only is asking you how to read an accompanying chart. Chart and graph questions are on most CLEP test and should be an easy free point.
- If you don't know the answer immediately, the new computer-based testing lets you mark questions and come back to them later if you have time.
- Read the wording carefully. Some words can give you hints to the right answer. There are no exceptions to an answer when there are words in the question such as

"always" "all" or "none". If one of the answer choices includes most or some of the right answers, but not all, then that is not the answer. Here is an example:

The primary colors include all of the following:

A) Red, Yellow, Blue, Green
B) Red, Green, Yellow
C) Red, Orange, Yellow
D) Red, Yellow, Blue
E) None of the above

Although item A includes all the right answers, it also includes an incorrect answer, making it incorrect. If you didn't read it carefully, were in a hurry, or didn't know the material well, you might fall for this.

- Make a guess on a question that you do not know the answer to. There is no penalty for an incorrect answer. Eliminate the answer choices that you know are incorrect. For example, this will let your guess be a 1 in 3 chance instead.

What Your Score Means

Based on your score, you may, or may not, qualify for credit at your specific institution. At University of Phoenix, a score of 50 is passing for full credit. At Utah Valley State College, the score is unpublished, the school will accept credit on a case-by-case basis. Another school, Brigham Young University (BYU) does not accept CLEP credit. To find out what score you need for credit, you need to get that information from your school's website or academic advisor.

You can score between 20 and 80 on any CLEP test. Some exams include percentile ranks. Each correct answer is worth one point. You lose no points for unanswered or incorrect questions.

Test Preparation

How much you need to study depends on your knowledge of a subject area. If you are interested in literature, took it in school, or enjoy reading then your studying and preparation for the literature or humanities test will not need to be as intensive as it would be for someone who is new to literature.

This book is much different than the regular CLEP study guides. This book actually teaches you the information that you need to know to pass the test. If you are particularly interested in an area, or feel like you want more information, do a quick search online. There is a lot you'll need to memorize. Almost everything in this book will be on the test. It is important to understand all major theories and concepts listed in the table of contents. It is also very important to know any bolded words.

Don't worry if you do not understand or know a lot about the area. If you study hard, you can complete and pass the test.

To prepare for the test, make a series of goals. Allot a certain amount of time to review the information you have already studied and to learn additional material. Take notes as you study-it will help you learn the material.

Legal Note

FLASHCARDS

This section contains flashcards for you to use to further your understanding of the material and test yourself on important concepts, names or dates. Read the term or question then flip the page over to check the answer on the back. Keep in mind that this information may not be covered in the text of the study guide. Take your time to study the flashcards, you will need to know and understand these concepts to pass the test.

Amendment 1

Amendment 2

Amendment 3

Amendment 4

Amendment 5

Amendment 6

Amendment 7

Amendment 8

Right of citizens to bear arms

Freedom of speech, of the press, and of religion. It also guarantees the rights of citizens to assemble and to petition the government for change

Protects citizens against "unreasonable searches and seizures"

That no one will be forced to house soldiers during peacetime

The rights of each citizens to a public trial

Protects citizens from being held without criminal charges, from having to testify against themselves, from being tried for the same crime twice (double jeopardy), and from being deprived of their rights without due process

Protects individuals from "cruel or unusual punishment" and from excessive bail

Guarantees the right to a jury trial in all cases involving more than $20

Amendment 9

Amendment 10

Amendment 11

Amendment 12

Amendment 13

Amendment 14

Amendment 15

Amendment 16

Gives power to the states to deal with anything that is not covered in the Constitution

Explains that even though some rights are not listed in the Constitution that does not mean individuals do not have those rights

Discusses the election process for President and Vice-president

Prohibits a citizen of one state from suing another state and prevents foreign individuals from suing states

Guarantees citizenship for people born in the United States or for people who go through the naturalization process

Abolishes slavery

Gives the government the right to collect income tax

Guarantees the rights of all men, regardless of color, to vote

Amendment 17

Amendment 18

Amendment 19

Amendment 20

Amendment 21

Amendment 22

Amendment 23

Amendment 24

Prohibits the making, selling and transporting of alcohol

ACE The CLEP

Allows for the direct election of Senators

ACE The CLEP

Deals with specifics of when presidential and congressional terms begin

ACE The CLEP

Gives women the right to vote

ACE The CLEP

Prevents a president from serving more than two terms

ACE The CLEP

Repeals Amendment XVIII (prohibition)

ACE The CLEP

Prohibits the charging of a poll tax

ACE The CLEP

Allows the District of Columbia the right to vote for president

ACE The CLEP

Amendment 25

Amendment 26

Amendment 27

What are the three branches of the government?

Which office requires the elected to be a natural born citizen?

Roe v. Wade covered what issue?

What was the decision of Roth v. United States?

Miranda v. Arizona

Allows people to vote at 18 instead of at 21

Discusses the succession of the president and vice-president

Legislative, Executive and Judiciary

Places a limit on how often Congress can vote to raise their pay

Determined that the government can not restrict a woman's ability to get an abortion after the first trimester

President

Stated that individuals who were arrested were supposed to be informed of their Constitutional rights

Determined that obscene material is not protected by the First Amendment

Baker v. Carr

Nix v. Hedden

Plussy v. Ferguson

Schenck v. United States

Pierce v. Society of Sisters of the Holy Names of Jesus and Mary

Lemon v. Kurtzman

Checks and balances

Marbury v. Madison

Determined that a tomato was classified as a vegetable, not a fruit

"one man, one vote"

ACE the CLEP

Limited the right of freedom of speech by stating that those rights did not apply to speech which created a "clear and present danger"

ACE the CLEP

Supported the idea of "separate but equal" in relation to segregation

ACE the CLEP

Established the Lemon Test which can be used to determine the Constitutionality of acts related to education and religion

ACE the CLEP

Due process

ACE the CLEP

Power of judicial review

ACE the CLEP

Having two parties compete for the same power to keep each in line

ACE the CLEP

Majority Leader

McCulloch v. Maryland

Gibbons v. Ogden

Dred Scott v. Sanford

Minority leader

Lochner v. New York

Korematsu v. United States

Brown v. Board of Education

1819. The Supreme Court ruled that Maryland did not have the right to tax the national bank. This promoted the supremacy of the Federal Government over state governments.

Second or principle deputy to the Speaker of the House.

1857. The Supreme Court ruled that Scott, a slave, had no right to sue in court because he was property.

1824. The Supreme Court affirmed that Congress had the right to regulate interstate commerce.

1905. The Supreme Court ruled that states could not limit hours worked a week because they couldn't interfere with a person's right to enter into an employment contract.

Leader of the party of opposition in the House.

1954. The Supreme Court declared that segregation in public schools was unconstitutional.

1944. The Supreme Court upheld the government's legal right to order Japanese citizens into internment camps during WWII.

Mapp v. Ohio

Whips

Ferguson v. Skrupa

Gideon v. Wainright

New York Times Co. v.
Sullivan

Supreme Court

Lobbyist

Regents of the University
of California v. Bakke

Deputies who hold an administrative position in each of the two main parties.

1961. The Supreme Court ruled that evidence obtained illegally was not admissible in court.

1963. The Supreme Court ruled that states are required to provide an attorney in criminal cases where the defendant cannot afford one.

1963. The Supreme Court ruled that Kansas had the right to determine the legality of "debt adjusting" because its legality was a legislative issue and not a judicial one.

Interprets the meaning of the Constitution and to applies it to actual situations.

1964. The Supreme Court ruled that actual malice must be proved for a printed criticism of a public official to be considered libel.

1978. The Supreme Court ruled that specified quota requirements based on race are unconstitutional.

Paid individuals whose job is to convince Congress members to vote one way or another on bills.

Hawaii Housing Authority v. Midkiff

Garcia v. San Antonio Transit Authority

Bowsher v. Synar

Bowers v. Hardwick

Constitutional Convention

Declaration of Independence

Federalism

Incumbent

1985. The Supreme Court affirmed that Congress has the right to impose minimum wage and overtime pay.

ACE The CLEP

1984. The Supreme Court affirmed the right of eminent domain in cases that would benefit the general public.

ACE The CLEP

1986. The Supreme Court upheld a law which made even private practice of homosexual acts illegal. The decision was later overturned.

ACE The CLEP

1986. The Supreme Court ruled that the Gramm-Rudman-Hollings Act was unconstitutional because it gave Congress the power to dismiss a member of the executive branch (the Comptroller General) though a process other than impeachment.

ACE The CLEP

A document passed by the Second Continental Congress in 1776 declaring the Independence of the 13 colonies and creation of the United States.

ACE The CLEP

A 1787 gathering in Independence Hall of representatives from the states which abolished the Articles of Confederation and wrote the Constitution. It created the federal system, three branches of government, two chamber legislation and 3/5 representation of slaves.

ACE The CLEP

A person who currently holds an office.

ACE The CLEP

A governmental system in which each citizen is subject to two governments. In the United States it’s the Federal and state government.

ACE The CLEP

Federalist Papers

Jim Crow Laws

Lemon Test

General Welfare Clause

Elastic Clause

Commerce Clause

We the People Clause

Supremacy Clause

A series of laws passed in the South after the Civil War which promoted segregation and racism.

A series of essays written by James Madison, John Jay and Alexander Hamilton in support of the passage of the Constitution.

Allows Congress to collect taxes to be used for the protection and general welfare of the citizens.

A set of requirements addressing legislative actions involving in religion.

Allows Congress to regulate trade with foreign nations and between individual states.

Allows Congress to pass all laws considered necessary and proper to perform their responsibilities. Also called the Necessary and Proper Clause.

Clause in the Constitution which declares that the Constitution and laws made by the Federal Government are the "supreme law of the land."

Another name for the Preamble to the Constitution.

Casework

Uniformity Clause

Reserved Powers Clause

Comity Clause

Guarantee Clause

Block Grant

Categorical Grant

Hard money contributions

Declares that all taxes must be uniform throughout the United States.

Congressional representative's efforts to help a constituent resolve a problem with the Federal bureaucracy.

Explains that citizens of one state have the same rights as citizens of other states.

Declares that powers and rights not given to Congress by the Constitution are held by the states and citizens.

Money awarded to a specific state by the Federal Government with general provisions on how it is to be used.

Guarantees Republican governments in each state.

Money legally donated to a specific candidate used for the purpose of campaigning. Maximum hard money donations are limited by law.

Money awarded to a specific state by the Federal Government with specific provisions and extensive restrictions on how it is to be spent.

Soft money contributions

Implied powers

Express powers

Establishment Clause

Writ of Habeas Corpus

Reapportionment

Gerrymandering

Realignment

Powers which a person takes to be implied or allowed due to the express powers they hold.

Money which is donated to political parties for “party building” purposes, often used by candidates to evade hard money limitations.

Prohibits Congress from passing laws “respecting an establishment of religion.”

Powers which are specifically stated or authorized by law.

Redistribution of Congressional seats after each census.

Protects individuals from being held without charge.

Shifts or changes in public opinion.

Redrawing voting districts to give one party or person an unfair advantage.

Bill of Rights

Legislative powers

Executive powers

Eminent domain

Litigation

Judicial powers

Mugwumps

Logrolling

The legislative branch is the sole law making body. They also declare war, impeach the president, and review presidential appointments.

The first ten Amendments to the United States Constitution.

The power of the government to take private property for public use after providing fair compensation.

The power of the executive branch lies with the President. His responsibility is to implement and enforce laws.

To oversee court systems, interpret the constitution, laws, and treaties and apply these interpretations to cases.

The process and legal proceedings of a lawsuit.

When two Congress members agree to vote for one another's unrelated bills.

Voters who do not identify themselves with any one party.

60102573R00087

Made in the USA
Lexington, KY
26 January 2017